An Accidental Hotelier

Roy A. Cook

An Accidental Hotelier

Copyright © 2017

Roy A. Cook

All rights reserved

ISBN-978-1542637572

ISBN-1542637570

Library of Congress Control Number: 2017900949
CreateSpace Independent Publishing Platform, North Charleston, SC

For information address The Source Guides, LLC, 1104 Oak Dr., Durango, CO 81301

Dedicated to Gwen, my wife, encourager, supporter and best friend.

Contents

Prologue

1   Stepping Stones

2   Opportunity Knocks

3   Old Fashioned or a Lesson in Decorum?

4   A Different Perspective

5   Paying My Dues

6   The Snoop?

7   Playing the Game

8   The Strike

9   The Spy

10   "You Just Don't Understand"

11   Decision Time

12   Words of Wisdom

14   Traditions

15   A Grand Opening Surprise

16   When in Doubt Call!

17   I've Got Pretty Legs

18   What a Deal!

19   False Imprisonment?

20 Five Minutes of Sheer Terror

21 Design Oversights?

22 Tanya Who?

23 The Union Knocks

24 Ouch!

25 Focusing on a Career Plan

26 Something Doesn't Seem Right

27 A Radical Change in Job Descriptions

28 Best Laid Plans

29 Dumpster Diving

30 The Fight

31 Sometimes it's not as Easy as You Think

32 When it Snows in the South

33 Don't Mess Around with Security

34 Wait Until You Hear from My Daddy!

35 Confidentiality Counts!

36 The Union Knocks Again

37 The Reward

Common Habits of Successful Hoteliers

[Type text]

Prologue

So, you think you want to be a hotelier? Have you even thought about the possibility of a career in the hotel business? Could this be the career for you? What, if anything, do you really know about this potential career? Let's peel back the curtain and look behind the scenes at the reality of this centuries old business and the people in it who say, "Welcome, come in, please be my guest."

When you hear the word, hotel, what comes to mind? Do you think about traveling, glamour, glitz, excitement, fun-filled weekends, vacations, business trips, or maybe living out of a suitcase? Or, do you think about jobs, opportunities, careers, long hours and maybe even working on weekends and holidays? Any of these thoughts would be correct because the hotel business is a twenty-four hour, seven day week people oriented business; and, with that comes the good and bad of working with people, both guests and co-workers.

Hotels, (broadly accommodations, hospitality and lodging), or inn keeping, have come to mean many different things to people through the years. Providing travelers with temporary shelter is an age-old profession that can be traced all the way from inn keepers as they were once known in biblical times to the managers of today's modern hotels. These manager or hoteliers, who by definition, are owners and operators of hotels, and all of their employees strive to ceremoniously say, "Welcome, come in; please be my guest."

Almost all of us, at some time, have had the opportunity to enjoy their hospitality. Our accommodations may have ranged anywhere from a limited-service roadside budget motel or a full-service airport hotel to a high-rise luxury downtown hotel or an all-inclusive resort, but no matter their size or location, they all shared one thing in common, a place to stay while away from home.

Because of the "fun-filled" perceptions and "pleasant memories" commonly associated with hotels, many individuals who say "I love people" or "I want to work in a fun environment" are attracted to both jobs and careers in this business. And, the demand for qualified management talent in this ever growing segment of the tourism industry never seems to be quenched.

In an effort to fill the staffing needs of hotels, thousands of college and university hospitality and tourism programs around the world have been developed for this specific purpose. These programs may differ in their content and focus, but they are all designed to provide the basic academic skills required for a successful career.

Most of these hospitality and tourism programs require some type of internship or practical work experience providing a realistic job preview of what it would really be like to work in the business. This exposure to reality is important. Even though a career in the hotel business may initially seem attractive, many students soon learn is that it is not for them. They quickly learn that people are not always nice and some of the jobs that must be performed on a daily basis are not all that pleasant. Many more, after just a little bit of experience, observe and quickly learn that individuals who thrive on providing customer service, problem-solving, and enjoy the self-fulfilling gratification of producing meaningful experiences, succeed and even become addicted to the hotel working environment. Still others discover over time that they don't have the temperament for the daily demands of the business.

Those that find themselves in a career in the hotel business say that there is nothing else like it. In fact, it has often been said that; "Once you have worked in the hotel business and enjoyed it, you will never get the desire to serve others out of your blood."

Most of the friends I made in college gained their business experience slowly, over time as they progressed through the rather predictable learning curves of their chosen careers or professions. Others, like me, who stumbled into a career in the hotel business, seemed to follow a random walk pushed by a rapid-fire succession of events creating unforgettable experiences. In comparison, there are few other jobs, maybe with the exception of food service, where you are challenged almost every day to think on your feet and deal with guests and employees. And, food service is a critical component of almost every large hotel operation. So anyone who has worked in a food service job should be mentally and emotionally prepared to work in the hotel business.

While a degree in tourism and hospitality can provide the preparation for an entry way into the business, there are many other experiences and degrees (as you will soon see) that can lead to successful hotel careers. You can learn a great deal from an internship or entry-level positions in hotels and restaurants, but, what is it really like to work in a supervisory or managerial position in the hotel business? Working in this business is nothing like the predictability found in an eight-to-five job, stuck in the confines of a "cookie cutter cubicle." As you will soon discover, as a supervisor or manager, you should learn to expect the unexpected.

Anyone with business experience, and especially hotel experience, will have a lot of "war stories" they can tell, but the stories you are about to read in this book are more than just war stories. From the hundreds of stories that can be told, from funny and sad to exciting and intriguing, the stories and the details surrounding these events have been especially selected with a purpose in mind. They have been selected not only to serve as realistic job previews for anyone considering a career in the hotel business, but they have also been selected because they provide learning opportunities for every aspiring hotelier no matter where they are in their career. Hopefully, these stories will spark your imagination. You may enjoy reading this book just for the fun of it, or, if you are planning a career in the hotel business, it will provide you with some valuable insights into the business.

An Accidental Hotelier

Story-telling is an age-old method of passing on knowledge by bringing reality into the learning experience. A story well told paints a vivid visual picture, sparking imagination and interest. In the tradition of story-telling focused on learning, this book is filled with a variety of situations encountered along a successful journey, filled with some stumbles, up the career ladder in the hotel industry.

The names of the people involved have been changed, basically to save them any embarrassment; everything else is told as it happened. You will soon discover that fact is much more interesting than fiction. To be fair, I have taken some very slight "poetic license" in some incidences to improve understanding, readability and flow.

As you journey through the pages of this book, hopefully, you will find yourself asking, what would you have done when faced with similar challenges and opportunities? Don't rush through to the end, instead take the time to contemplate the facts in each of the incidents, placing yourself in the situation and then considering how you might have responded. Focus on each set of events, recognizing that each situation is a learning opportunity that could pave the way for your own personal career growth.

Think of each situation as a potential realistic job preview. With that in mind, always ask yourself the following two questions. First, what can I learn from these experiences that I can apply to my own career success no matter where I work? Second, would I enjoy working in this type of fast-paced people-oriented service business where these types of incidents actually happen? It is my hope that when you complete this journey, you will have enjoyed many vicarious learning experiences, gained valuable personal insights and come away better prepared to create your own career success. So, let's begin the journey by looking at the stepping stones paving the path toward becoming a hotelier.

1
Stepping Stones

Before we start down this convoluted career path story, you need a little bit of background information on the person who is the focus of these stories. I grew up with two very supportive parents and two older siblings, both with very divergent and ultimately different career choices. There was nothing really earth-shattering about my early school days; some awards, leadership positions, but mainly just a lot of fun. I enjoyed sports, but you could never accuse me of being athletic.

As high school graduation approached, there was very little guidance. I did briefly consider a trade, but as a first generation college student there was really no question what I would be doing. All the kids in my family went to college! When it came to a choice of which college, course of study and degree, I was given some very specific guidance. Go to college and get a degree! It didn't matter what type of degree, just get a degree, you will need a degree to succeed. My dad never encouraged any of us to follow in his footsteps, but he had seen the importance of college degrees in his line of work and wanted all of us to get a degree. So off to college I went and this is where the story begins.

For some, getting a college degree is just a rite-of-passage, something to be endured. For others, college presents unplanned opportunities that create life-changing experiences. One thing is true for every graduate: by the time you have earned your degree, you will have experienced and learned to survive and endure under just about every style of classroom management imaginable. Some of your professors were caring, others were tyrants. Some of them probably didn't even seem to know that you were in their class, but others were truly inspirational.

You learned to adapt to different teaching styles. Many of the same comments could be made about our classmates and friends. An ever changing set of classmates and team mates on projects and exercises was good training for dealing with the wide variety of co-workers and management styles you will encounter during your career.

Exploring the world through the comfort of the college classroom can place you in situations where your emotions can range all the way from bored to challenged, and frustrated to excited; and, at times, all of these and more emotions can be experienced in the same course on the same day. Every semester, you find yourself in a familiar, yet slightly different setting where you are exposed to new ideas. Questions are raised and sometimes answered; new passions are sparked and fanned into flames of interest and action; others are snuffed out, and, at times, doors are opened to new adventures and avenues for future exploration. It will be more of the same when you start and progress through your career, or more likely, careers. If you choose a career in the hotel business or find yourself entering a career in the hotel business later in life, prepare to be bored, challenged, satisfied and amazed each new day!

For most college students, life's business experiences are gained slowly after graduation, over time as they progress through one or more careers seeking that "perfect fit." Others, like me who stumbled into a career, seem to follow a random walk pushed by a rapid-fire succession of events that force us to rise to challenges beyond our years and experiences.

There is much to be learned from the classroom. Textbooks and lectures provide valuable knowledge for enjoying the world around you and for analyzing and solving problems. Group exercises and team projects help to refine this knowledge while providing practice in dealing with a variety of personalities ranging from "over achievers" to "social loafers." Education, as you already know, is an important building block for personal growth, as it provides a necessary, but not sufficient foundation for success in the business world. However, there is more to managerial success than simply a sound educational foundation. The other important building block for success in business, especially the hotel business, is experience. When experience, gained either personally or vicariously, is added to a solid education, the foundation is being set in place for a successful career.

The hotel industry may be the perfect crucible for combining education and experience to develop managerial talent: in this fast-paced and rapidly growing industry that is always in need of managerial talent. Many aspiring young managers find themselves in situations which may seem to be beyond their training and experience, but they are required to respond. Sometimes they respond correctly and sometimes they don't; but always, they grow. You may find yourself in similar situations that test your ability to "use your wits and think fast on your feet" as you gain experience and climb the career ladder.

There is also even more to be learned from the realities of on-the-job experiences. Every time you encounter someone you respect as a supervisor or mentor along this path, pay attention to how they handle themselves and others. Learn from their examples and model your behaviors for success. Each of the incidents you encounter as you turn the pages of this book has been selected from a variety of daily events and thought-provoking experiences that capture both the typical and not-so-typical situations facing a manager in the hotel business. It is only through experiences like these that managers in the hotel business learn to deal with people: guests, employees (team members), and suppliers (purveyors). You will also discover some interesting insights into the hotel business in FYI's related to specific situations.

Think about each situation, considering your own experiences in dealing with people in a business setting. How have you reacted to your own successes and failures in those situations? If you have not already done so, learn to be humble in your successes and realize that almost always, others contributed to your success and should be thanked for doing so. Perhaps even more important, learn to grow from your mistakes and failures. How you respond to these mistakes and failures may be even more important in your personal growth and career progression than your successes.

It is easy to bask in the glory of your successes, but your mistakes and failures are a different story. Mistakes and failures are painful and often fill a person with both fear and shame. Try as we might to avoid them, to some degree everyone fails and makes mistakes. In fact, every successful business person will tell you they have made many mistakes during their careers. Whether your responses to your mistakes turn out to be stepping stones to future successes, or have negative career impacts, depends on how you handle them. Those who are successful, admit and learn from their mistakes; correct them when possible, apologize when appropriate, ask for forgiveness, and move forward.

As you will soon see from the stories told through the incidents and episodes in this book, many valuable life lessons can be learned from a wide variety of industry-specific experiences in a very compressed time frame. What follows happened in just a few short years following graduation. Hopefully, reading and thinking about these experiences will contribute to your own success.

With that in mind, what can be learned from your early experiences?

- Graduating from college is a major milestone in your life. Be proud of your accomplishment in achieving this milestone and your ability to work under differing types of-supervision. Showcase these skills to

demonstrate your ability to adapt and accomplish goals in any type of setting, especially as you begin your career.
- Formal education may be an important stepping stone to your career, but there is no substitute for experience.
- Imitation is the best form of flattery, so flatter those who taught you by demonstrating what you learned and imitate the behaviors of those you admire.
- Be cautious, measure what people say: study, observe, and question. Always remember, that any time you are dealing with people, their past behaviors are the best predictor of their future behavior. People's actions often speak louder than their words.
- Look for inspiration from those around you and, in return, share your knowledge and experiences by instructing and mentoring others through your own stories about how these events have shaped your own career.

With all of that said, even with well made plans and preparation, there is no telling where you might find yourself in the future. As the events in the next chapter demonstrate, be prepared to respond when opportunity knocks.

2

Opportunity Knocks

My sister-in-law has always said that I am the quintessential businessman. She ought to know, since she has known me since age 10. I'm never quite sure whether that moniker is a backhanded insult or a compliment, but I resemble it! I am fascinated with everything about the world of business and will talk about business subjects, especially hospitality and tourism subjects, with anyone willing to listen.

It is probably not too difficult to imagine that I was one of the few college freshmen who was excited about being in a classroom with 120 other eager and not so eager students in an Introduction to Business class at a state university. College was interesting, but there were a lot of required classes that held little interest and seemed like drudgery. When I finally got through the dreaded required classes and into my major, school all of a sudden became exciting. It was three years from that Introduction to Business class to my senior year (yes, I graduated in three and a half years, worked part-time and even took off one summer to earn some very needed extra money) where my story of embarking on the path to becoming a hotelier begins.

I was living off-campus with my roommate, Doug. During our second semester together, he told me that his dad was coming to visit and he wanted to make sure that everything would be "ship shape" when he arrived. Cleaning and straightening up the apartment didn't take long. After that task was accomplished, being studious was high on my list of things to do, as I had a paper due in my Capstone Senior class at the end of the week.

When Doug's dad showed up, I was sitting at the kitchen table, intently focused on writing the first draft of a case analysis. My favorite desk, even to this day and with this book, has always been the kitchen table, and my research was spread all over the table.

Looking up from my work, there stood Doug's dad in the kitchen doorway. I got up, introduced myself and we firmly shook hands, a typical Southern behavior, and, as I would learn later, a common practice of business etiquette for both men and women. After the typical pleasantries, he asked me, "What are you up to?" "Well, I'm writing up the financial analysis portion of a case study." He then asked, "Mind if I talk with you about your analysis?"

We immediately got into the details of my analysis. He was very interested in what I was doing, knew what he was talking about, as far as I was concerned, and, to my surprise, was very enthusiastic about the topics. We talked about trend analysis, common-sized financial statements, liquidity and profitability ratios, financial leverage and more. Doug quickly lost interest, but the conversation with his dad continued on for another couple of hours as we discussed what I had learned in my classes and my life experiences.

At the end of the evening, Doug rejoined us and I said my good-byes. His dad's parting comment was, "Be sure to send me your resume when you graduate." I said, "I'd be glad to, but I'm headed to graduate school." To that he replied, "Well, don't forget to send it to me when you finish graduate school."

The next day, I asked Doug in passing, "What does your dad do?" "He's the President of a hotel company." "Public or private," I asked. "Public, over-the-counter," was Doug's reply. "Can I get a copy of the annual report?" Doug said his dad probably had a copy with him, and he would be happy to ask for one.

I never saw his dad again on that visit, but Doug did get a copy of the annual report for me. Sure enough, there was a picture of Doug's dad accompanying the Letter to the Shareholders in the front of the report. He really was the President of the company!

* * *

Entering into a Master of Business Administration (MBA) program created a whole new set of learning opportunities. Although it is not typical to enter an MBA program straight out of an undergraduate program, I had owned my own small business and been working part-time in some very responsible positions for many years. My professors in graduate school were fantastic and several became my mentors! They introduced me to the importance of writing and assisted me in publishing two journal articles while still a student. In addition, I gained a great deal of self-confidence as I attended the program on a graduate assistantship that required me to teach two courses each semester. You had better be self-confident, a good communicator, and organized when, at 21 years of age, you step in front of business classes filled with sophomores and juniors close to your same age.

A short year and a half later, as graduation approached, placement was on everyone's mind. I remembered that chance encounter in the kitchen with Doug's dad and his admonition, "Don't forget to send me your resumé when you finish graduate school." I heeded that request and sent Doug's dad a cover letter and resumé. To my surprise, I got a call the next week from the Vice President of Human Resources asking when I would be available for an on-site interview.

After discussing logistics, we set a date. Shortly afterwards, an airline ticket confirmation arrived along with hotel and rental car confirmation numbers and directions from the airport to the company's flagship hotel, which was also the location of the corporate office. Following two days of whirlwind interviews and a job offer, I was headed back for my final eight weeks of school, teaching, final exams, grading and graduation.

This was my second job offer, but the first job offer paled into insignificance at the thought of working in a corporate office position at the headquarters of a small publicly traded hotel company. You'll learn more about the specifics of the position when you turn the page to the next chapter.

So, two letters were written. The first was to accept the hotel's offer. The second one was to thank the other organization for their offer, wish them well, and inform them that after careful consideration, I was accepting an opportunity with another employer.

Little did I know at the time I said yes to the hotel offer that this was the first step on a whirlwind career that turned into a journey. So, what can we learn from these chance encounters?

- Show confidence through positive body language. One simple way to do this is to always have a firm, but not bone-crushing, handshake, and extend that hand of friendship to everyone you meet!
- Pay attention and listen closely to anyone who shows an interest in you and your career success. You never know where those encounters may lead. They can happen in school, internships or on the job; if you keep your eyes open, they will present themselves often and from a variety of sources as you move through your career.
- Always treat everyone you encounter, no matter who they are, with respect. This means everyone, from the custodians and housekeepers to administrative assistants and not just superiors and corporate executives.
- You never know when opportunity might knock, so always be ready to answer the door and find out what

lies on the other side. When an opportunity presents itself, take the time to explore and respond with a timely follow-up.

The entry into my career path may have been different than others in the hotel business, but my experiences from that point on may not be all that different from anyone else in the business. See what you think as you look at one of the "time honored" lessons about the hotel business presented in the next chapter.

3

Old Fashioned or a Lesson in Decorum?

Taking that hotel company job found me moving from the sunny South to the frozen North, in January, no less. This truly was a life changing experience. Growing up in the South, summer was a time of sun, fun, and anticipation. The sun was always there and the fun and outdoor play time or chores began as the school ended for the year. The shoes came off; bare feet or flip flops became the "foot wear of choice" and a swimming suit or shorts rounded out the summer wardrobe. For a young boy it couldn't have gotten any better. No one even thought about slowing down on the fun until the last rays of sunlight grudgingly faded from the sky. More importantly, as each day of summer passed, the anticipation grew for one of our family's last big summer hurrahs – the road trip!

My dad liked to drive and living in South Texas meant you had to drive to get almost anywhere. Our final days of summer always meant family vacation time. Some of these vacations were camping trips to nearby state parks, but others were road trip adventures. When we "hit the road," it usually found us traveling to see one of the nation's national parks with an obligatory stop to tour any state capitol we happened to be near. Mom believed in education and visiting state capitols was considered to be a fundamental foundation of a good education.

For me, one of the highlights of these trips was staying in a motel (never a hotel), but a small "mom and pop" operation or a franchised roadside motel, usually after two or three days of camping. Hot showers, air conditioning, glasses wrapped in plastic, ice buckets, little bars of soap, and a swimming pool were Nirvana for a young boy. I soon began collecting motel directories and planning possible stops as soon as our next destination was announced.

Little did I know that several years later, a career in the hotel business was about to unfold, and I had never even stayed in a hotel. The only time I had set foot in a hotel was for a Sunday brunch on a very special occasion. Do you remember that chance encounter with the president of a hotel chain that led me to apply for and accept a job in the corporate office? Being fresh out of school with an MBA concentrating in finance, convinced me that I had "all the knowledge in the world" and there was nothing more to learn. I had passed my oral defense, the final requirement for my degree, and I truly was ready to "conquer the world of business." I was sure I knew it all, and it was time to show off my finance and accounting knowledge.

An Accidental Hotelier

Family vacations and formal education were now just memories; it was time to begin my career. From the first day on the job, there were challenging projects like analyzing investments for the company's portfolio, creating pro-forma financial statements, and performing basic research for potential projects. These were all "glamorous" tasks, but there were also the mundane tasks like costing menus and performing basic internal audit procedures. All of this took place in the corporate offices located on one floor of a massive downtown destination hotel.

I had arrived! I was working in a "comfortable office complex" that just happened to be located in a hotel, but it didn't seem like I was in the hotel business. Everyone working in the corporate office entered the office area through a separate entrance apart from the hotel and most of us almost never had any daily contact with hotel customers. Although we seemed to be far removed from the realities of daily activities in the hotel that surrounded us, we were often reminded that we were a key part of a business dedicated to serving the guests who paid our salaries and the bills. That didn't matter; it was a business and I was using the knowledge and skills acquired in my MBA. I was proving my worth!

* * *

My first dose of reality about being a "hotelier" came during a sweltering hot August day. The air conditioning for the office part of the hotel complex "conked" out mid-morning. This may not have been a story worth telling except that every management person in the hotel followed a strict dress code. Coats and ties and dresses or pant suits for women were mandatory at work. We catered to a very discriminating clientele, so as we were told, on the chance that a guest interaction may occur, we dressed the part to make our guests feel comfortable and respected.

By mid-afternoon, the temperature and humidity had risen to create what seemed like an unbearable "sweat box" and the word around the office was that the air conditioning wouldn't be up and running again until the next day. As far as I was concerned, it was time for the suit coats, which had now become a personal sauna, to come off. So, off came my coat and I even loosened my tie.

Now, sitting comfortably at my desk in my shirt sleeves with my tie loosened, one of my co-workers looked over at me and said, "You'd better put your coat back on." I looked at her and said, "You've got to be kidding!" To which she replied, "Don't forget the dress code."

Don't forget the dress code? What a silly comment to make! I looked around the office and sure enough everyone was still dressed according to the dress code. I wondered why anyone would care in this heat. As far as I was concerned, there was no sense in being uncomfortable under these conditions! Is this the end of story? Well, not quite.

The President of the company had a habit of practicing "Management by Walking Around." And today was one of those days when he was practicing the concept. As he passed by my desk, it didn't even seem like he even broke his stride, but he did pause long enough to say, "See me in my office."

I finished the task I was doing and got up to head to his office. Once again, my co-worker said, "You'd better put on your coat." You may have also noticed by now, that we were very formal in the office, a practice that was also followed in the hotel in deference to our guests; no first names were used, ever! Showing respect for our guests who were paying "top dollar" for their accommodations and services was paramount to our focus on customer service. We were just in the habit of always using last names when addressing each other. As I headed away from my desk, I once again shot my concerned co-worker a "you've got to be kidding" look.

Arriving at the president's office, I told the administrative assistant that I had been asked to come to his office. I thought I was a fast learner. But, the next part of this episode will soon convince you that during the early part of my career, I wasn't quick to pick on the importance of corporate culture. His assistant gave me a somber look and simply said, "He's expecting you, but you should really go back and get your coat before you go in." My reply was just as simple, "That's okay; it's way too hot." And with that exchange, I stepped through and into his office.

Boy oh boy, in hindsight, what a mistake that was! I was immediately on the receiving end of a long and very stern lecture on decorum in the hotel business. I soon learned what everyone else already knew; we were all to act like ladies and gentlemen as we had an image to uphold for our guests, no matter whether they saw us or not. The bottom line of this very uncomfortable lecture was very straight-forward: "You will learn to sweat like a gentleman." Duly humbled and slightly bowed, I headed back to my desk and donned my coat just like every other miserable person in the office and endured the almost unbearable heat until the work day was over.

All my well-intended, helpful, co-worker said as we left for the day was "I told you so." I knew by the events of the day that I was now officially in the hotel business and I was a lot more willing to listen to those little tidbits of advice proffered by those who were already part of this business and wanted me to succeed. Just like I had discovered at every other job I had in the past, it was time to once again listen to potential mentors.

Do you think this story may be a bit over the top? Think again, and remember Ritz-Carlton's famous slogan: "We are ladies and gentlemen, serving ladies and gentlemen." Is there more to be learned from this episode? The answer is, yes.

- Management by Walking Around is a practice that keeps managers informed about what is happening in their organizations and workers on their toes. It also provides opportunities for both supervisors and managers to stay in touch. More importantly, it works!
- Every organization has a culture. Observe it, learn it, and do everything possible to fit in and become part of it. You may work in a casual setting, one that requires uniforms, or one like I entered that is very formal. Don't be surprised by formality in the hotel business, as many hotels, especially up-scale hotels in major metropolitan centers, are very formal.

- Enjoy your work, but pay attention to and fit into the culture of the organization. Make sure you observe expected dress codes and behaviors on the job -- they exist for a reason. If the culture of the organization is "not for you," and you find yourself being uncomfortable with the culture, move on until you find a comfortable fit.
- It might seem old fashioned, but the hotel business is built on traditions. Take time to learn these traditions. As a first step, begin by always showing respect and addressing guests and superiors on a more formal basis as either Mr. or Ms. until asked to do otherwise.
- You never know who will give you valuable career advice, so listen carefully to everyone, especially co-workers who want you to succeed.

Learning the culture of an organization is a continuous process. As the next chapter shows, you need to take advantage of every opportunity presented to you, as it may change your perspective about your employer.

4

A Different Perspective

There were two of us who started working in the corporate office at the same time. The other person, Jim, was also hired into a new trainee type position that had been created in the accounting and finance area. Like me, he had several tasks that had been planned for his position, but we ended up working on some of the same projects. We both spent time with the Vice President of Human Resources on our first day getting a general overview of the corporation and the hotel where we would be working, but that was the extent of our orientation.

After a few weeks on the job, Jim and I went through the standard orientation program designed for hotel employees. You may wonder why it took so long to be scheduled for an official orientation program. The answer was, formal orientation was only scheduled when new employees were being brought on-board to the hotel, and this was the first time there was a group of new employees. Turnover was low in this hotel, which is an oddity in the hotel business, but this hotel was considered by everyone you talked to in the community to be a great place to work.

Orientation was scheduled for half a day, and the program was designed to welcome everyone on-board and make us feel like we were part of the "team." We covered all the basics from company history and operating philosophies to where and when to scan our identification badges for recording our hours, to benefits and paydays.

As part of the process, we were welcomed by the General Manager (GM) of the hotel and introduced to several other key managers who told us about their departments and the importance of everyone working together to serve our guests. We were a small group; a busser and coffee shop server, two housekeepers, an electrician, Jim and me. Jim and I didn't really seem to fit in, as we the only management type persons in the orientation group and we didn't have actual jobs in the hotel. It didn't seem like much of what were learning applied to us other than getting a general overview of the hotel.

Finally, before we were to be greeted by our respective supervisors, we were given a grand tour of the hotel by someone from the Human Resources Department. I had never seen the entire hotel, so this part of the orientation was really fascinating. We started with the front of the house departments like the bell stand, concierge, the front desk, each of the restaurants and bars, banquet and meeting rooms and other public areas. Then we moved to the behind-the-scenes back of the house departments like the kitchen, bakery, dry and cold storage areas, dish room, housekeeping, maintenance, accounting and reservations. We didn't see everything, but it was obvious that a large hotel like this one was a major operation, and there were literally employees everywhere!

After the tour, Jim and I went back to the corporate office as our other new team members were greeted by their supervisors and headed off to begin their first day with a little on-the-job training. Having been immersed in basic accounting work and general "number crunching" type projects, orientation was definitely a change of pace and it gave me a better idea of the type of business I was in, from an employee rather than a guest perspective.

Although there were many opportunities to interact with different managers and see other parts of the hotel on various assignments, these encounters were always brief, and then it was once again back to the office. After a few months on the job, when returning from lunch in the cafeteria, the GM asked if Jim and I if we would like to walk the property (another term used by hoteliers is house) with him. Jim said he had work to do and returned to the office. I jumped at the chance and took the opportunity to walk and talk with the GM.

We hadn't gotten very far along with our "walk" until he bent down and picked up a scrap of paper. Not too much further along on this walk, he took out a small notebook from his pocket and wrote down a comment about a dent in the wall that looked like it may have been created by a hit from some type of cart. All the time we were walking, he was asking me about my thoughts on the hotel business and sharing a few stories about his career in the business. As we looked in one of the ballrooms, he again pulled out his little notebook and made a note about one of the light bulbs being out in one of the four massive chandeliers (there were hundreds of bulbs in these chandeliers) in the room. Another note was made when he discovered a room service tray on a guest room floor in the alcove where the vending and ice machines were located.

The whole tour took maybe thirty minutes and the time flew by as we just walked and talked. When we finished, or I thought we had finished, the GM asked me what I had seen. My comments where about big picture things. He said this was okay, but I needed to learn to look at the hotel from a different perspective. He said, "To think about the hotel as your home and look at it from the eyes of our guests." Pay attention to the little things and then they will not turn into big things.

Jim and I both had other opportunities to walk the property with some of the other managers. Although Jim wasn't interested in the hotel side of things and wanted to focus on his office tasks, I took advantage of all of these walks. They were all basically the same; everyone paid attention to the details. One other thing was also very noticeable during this "walk." He said "hello" and called every hotel employee we passed by name. Sometimes he even stopped and chatted for a brief moment. It was easy to call someone by name as we all wore nametags, but the conversations seemed to be personal. It wasn't long before I was noticing little things like an empty drink cup on the sidewalk outside the hotel or a burnt out light bulb and started calling employees by name. I also noticed that Jim put in his eight hours and left. We were working for the same company, but our interests were different.

Things were starting to change, I was beginning to look at the hotel business differently each passing day. If you want to be part of the hotel business:

- Develop the ability to look at every aspect of your hotel through the eyes of your guests. Think about how they view and use your property.
- Pay attention to details and take care of the hotel like it is your own. Even something as small as a scrap of paper or a stray cigarette butt can send a message to your guests that you don't care.
- Everyone who works in a hotel is important and there is no better way to recognize someone than to call them by their name.
- There is a lot to be learned from just walking around and observing. Depending on the size of your property walk all of both the inside and outside every single day, once, if not multiple times.
- Every time you are offered an opportunity to learn or gain a new experience, take it, even if it means you may have to put in a few more hours of work. And, do it cheerfully!

By this time you might think that I should have learned all of the basics of the business. However, the next chapter shows that there was still a lot to be learned about being a hotelier.

5

Paying My Dues

It wasn't long after the "Learn to Sweat Like a Gentleman" incident that I got a call to make an appointment with the Vice President of Operations. He seemed like an easy-going gentleman that I had interacted with on several occasions, especially when working on feasibility studies for remodeling projects, new venue concepts or proposed changes to service offerings. However, this request for a meeting didn't seem like the previous ones.

When I arrived at his office at the appointed time (wearing my coat), I excused myself as I knocked and then stepped into his office. He was meeting with the Vice President of Human Resources, and I said, "Sorry for interrupting, I'll wait outside until you're finished." This comment was met with a "No, no, please come in. We've been expecting you." Groaning to myself, I silently thought, "I hope this isn't more about the coat incident. Enough is enough, especially with the teasing I'd been getting."

It was with a great deal of relief that the conversation began with compliments on how well I was doing and questions about how I liked my job. Then the conversation quickly segued into hotel topics like the night audit, the front desk, housekeeping, restaurants, lounges, kitchens, sanitation, and more. I should have seen that the trap was being set, but I was having too much fun just chatting with two vice presidents. How many other people in my position as a "newbie" to the company got to rub elbows with the top brass? It must have been my MBA! They were probably interested in my thoughts on some important new project!

I couldn't have been more mistaken about my importance. Not much later in my career and a fact that you will soon discover in the hospitality business, as I was already learning on my "walks," it is a common practice for hotel executives to interact with employees at every level of the organization on an almost daily basis.

That ego bubble was soon burst when the trap was sprung with one pointed statement and then a question from the Vice President of Human Resources: "We've been studying your resume and work history and haven't noticed any practical experience in the hotel business. Do you want to make a career for yourself in the hotel business?" They had set me up perfectly; and I had taken the bait! Snap! They had me when I said, "Yes." The door had closed and there was no turning back. I soon learned that everyone from front line supervisors to senior management had spent some time performing one or more hourly (non-exempt) line employees' duties at some time during their careers. Having performed these duties was considered to be a "rite of passage" or said another way, it was considered to be an expected way of "paying your dues" in order to move up the career ladder in the hospitality business.

Shortly after this meeting, a four-week training schedule was put together that would introduce me to the "real side" of the hotel business. It started with a one week rotation in night audit on the 11:00 p.m. to 7:00 a.m. shift. This first assignment made a lot of sense as the starting point for my hotel education as I often performed random audits on different portions of the night auditors' reports. Before we go any further with this training adventure, you need to know that I was still responsible for performing my daily duties in the office in addition to "learning the business." Little did I know that these long hours would prepare me for the work experiences that lay ahead.

* * *

The setting where my training was taking place was in a very large, inspiring, classic, pristinely maintained downtown destination hotel, complete with multiple restaurants and lounges and a variety of meeting and banquet rooms. As I've mentioned before, the corporate offices were also located in the hotel, but they were just like any other office. The hotel was big, and always seemed to be bustling with activities, sights, and sounds. It was alive and I found myself becoming part of it!

After one week on the night audit, I rotated to the afternoon, 3:00 p.m. to 11:00 p.m. shift on the front desk. This was an opportunity to become familiar with reservations, the vocabulary of room types and rates, managing inventory and the art of interacting with all types of guests. They came to the front desk in all types of moods, which created an interesting challenge for making each one of them feel like they were the center of our attention, reinforcing the importance of our focus on customer service. Other than learning procedures and routines, there was nothing special about this rotation except for the employees who quickly became a part of my life. They were all long-term employees and they all seemed to love what they were doing. Their positive attitudes towards guests and their passion for service was special.

The third week of the training rotation found me in the housekeeping department. After a week of cleaning toilets, cleaning up other peoples' messes and stripping and making one bed after another, I was convinced that no one works harder in a hotel than housekeepers. You try cleaning up the messes left in fifteen rooms and making perfectly square corners on every bed for five days in a row and see what you think. Some of the housekeepers I worked alongside had been doing that type of work for the hotel for over twenty years! It was obvious from the pride in their work that these housekeepers were very special people.

My final rotation took me to the kitchen. This rotation began with the pastry department that started work at 3:00 a.m. and progressed through purchasing and all of the stations, ending in stewarding. I even spent time with the dish washing crew that never left until at least an hour after the restaurants closed or the final banquet was bussed. On one night I closed with this crew; we did not leave the hotel until 1:00 a.m. the next morning! Returning to my regular job duties on the next morning at 8:00 a.m. made for a couple of long days.

While in the kitchen, I got a very brief exposure to everything from menu planning and ordering to preparations to fine dining and mass production for banquets to stewarding and inventory control. One week was an eye-opener for not only how intricate the rhythm, timing and flow of food service can be; but it was also obvious that a week's worth of experience was only scratching the surface of the complexities of food service.

FYI

There are a lot of people working behind-the-scenes in a large full-service hotel. Some of these people, like housekeepers and maintenance personnel, you may see, but others like accounts and laundry personnel you may never see because their jobs truly keep them behind-the-scenes. There are many others you will never see, unless you work in the business or get up very early in the morning. One example of a really hard working crew that is seldom seen but always appreciated is the pastry team. Set your alarm for 2:00 a.m. if you want to work with this group, because by 3:00 a.m. they will already be hard at work creating their culinary wonders for the day!

After four weeks, I was hooked. What other business could I work in that offers the experience of instant gratification from providing a service and then immediately seeing the satisfaction it produces? It was easy to see why so many of those involved in the hotel business found their work to be so satisfying. It was also easy to see why some people don't enjoy the never-ending demands of guests or the demands on their time.

So, what knowledge can we gather from these learning experiences?

- If you are going to succeed in the hotel business, you need to understand it. Experiencing what employees do at every level and in and in every job is invaluable to knowing the details of what it takes to make a service organization like a hotel function properly. Think about it this way, how can you be a leader if you are not willing to do the job?
- In a service oriented business like a hotel, it is the people (employees / team members) who make the difference. Get to know everyone with whom you work and greet them by name each and every day.
- The hotel business is exciting, if not, intoxicating. It has been said that once you get the hotel business into your blood, you can never get it out!

- Take advantage of every opportunity to gain practical experience through part-time jobs, shadowing opportunities, special assignments, and internships. Working hard to learn the basics of the business, especially while still in school, will go a long way toward advancing your career.
- In the hotel business, no matter how far up the career ladder you advance, remember that you are still in the business of serving others, both employees and customers, and that you will always continue to pay your dues every day, but there will always be opportunities to experience the satisfaction of providing quality customer service!

This introduction to the hotel business was brief, but it was a harbinger of more unknown in-depth training yet to come. However, there was another more immediate assignment that was just around the corner. There may be no other all-encompassing assignment that will bring home the reality of how much there is to learn in the hotel business and how important every function is than being placed in the role of an internal auditor, as you will see in the next chapter.

6

The Snoop?

I was the first MBA hired into the organization and this always brought up the question of, was an MBA really important? After being on the job for a few months, and hearing that question more than one time, I began to question the value of this advanced degree myself. Then I found out that hiring me had been the idea of the President. His thought had been to hire someone to assist the Treasurer, Corporate Secretary, and the Controller with investment decisions and special projects.

As a home base, I was assigned to work for the Assistant Controller, Fred, (when we worked together he always insisted that I call him by his first name), and he was charged with keeping me busy; helping out with routine tasks when I was not working on special assignments. The projects the President had envisioned for my position soon proved to take up a very small portion of my work week as they were relatively easy to complete and keeping me busy always seemed to pose a problem.

I'll never know whether the next assignments were designed to get me out of the office so Fred could quit having to find things for me to do, or if they were just additional "learning experiences" to enhance my career and value to the company. Whatever the reasons, I soon found myself traveling on week-long assignments to different properties in the hotel chain conducting internal audits.

The importance of conducting internal audits was a concept that had been discussed in the classroom, but actually performing an internal audit was much different than reading about it. In brief, an internal auditor reviews operational performance against established metrics, reviews the adequacy of financial procedures and controls, and makes recommendations for possible improvements in all of these areas. Serving as an internal auditor provides an opportunity to take an in-depth look at every aspect of the business.

These internal audits conformed to a prescribed format established and communicated by Fred and were explained to the General Managers (GMs) and their staff as performance check-ups, to highlight what was going well and what could be improved. In reality they were a program designed to uncover operating deficiencies and slack financial procedures with an eye toward improving operating efficiencies and profitability. Since I was new to the corporation, the real question for me when I headed out on each of these assignments was, how would I be received upon arrival?

Going through the audit checklist and observing operations would be simple. The audits were straightforward from a procedural standpoint, as performance metrics had been established and agreed to by all of the GMs, but the process was a little bit more difficult from a human relations perspective. In all fairness to the GMs and their staff, since this was the first time this particular procedure had been used in the chain, there was a great deal of skepticism. In reality, no matter how these visits had been billed and described prior to my arrival, when I did arrive, I was considered to be a "snoop" and viewed with a respectable amount of suspicion.

Needless to say, my visits were never accompanied with a warm welcome. Each of the GMs had grown accustomed to meeting annually with the corporate staff for budgeting purposes, establishing performance metrics, hosting respective staff members to sort through operational questions, and providing suggestions for improvements in their areas of expertise. And, although at times considered to be bothersome, preparing reports and sending in weekly performance statistics providing comparisons to budgeted goals was an accepted way of life. However, this was the first time they had been subjected to up-close and personal scrutiny. This was an extra layer of oversight that they seemed to consider to be an "intrusion" from the corporate office; and, therefore, the process was not welcomed.

They considered me to be an outsider who was meddling in their business, and were quick to tell me so. Remember, a GM is a true hotelier and should really be considered the equivalent to a manager of a small city overseeing a multi-million dollar budget. They are responsible for meeting the payroll for hundreds of employees, serving as host or hostess to thousands of transient guests, serving as the face of the company to the local community, as well as performing a variety of other duties. Their responsibilities require them to be in-charge and make decisions every day; they are the boss. They are accustomed to being in charge. Serving in the role of an internal auditor, I was not one of their employees, but I needed their cooperation and support to be successful in completing my work.

One thing you should know about any audit process is that if you look long enough, you can always find a discrepancy or a more efficient way to complete a task. But, before we go any further with this episode, let's take time for a little digression about me, the internal auditor, and one of my more memorable auditing engagements.

* * *

By the time I set off on my internal audit assignments, I had reached the ripe old age of 24. So here you have a very young person, with extremely limited operational experience, an MBA in a culture where that was an oddity, being sent out to review the operations of seasoned GMs. Do I need to say any more?

One particular incident in the course of completing one of my audits will highlight the significance of my lack of operational experience. This audit assignment was at a hotel located close to the Canadian border. I arrived in February to conduct this audit, and immediately noticed four things. First, it was bitter cold and felt even colder as the wind never stopped howling. Second, the sun never peeked through the clouds. Third, liquor sales were way above normal when compared to similarly sized properties and the bar was always busy from opening until closing time. Fourth, and a bit more curious, there were two snowmobiles on the property's inventory of capital assets. Having grown up in South Texas, I immediately identified the snowmobiles as being frivolous and decided to suggest that they be sold.

When mentioning my idea about disposing of the snowmobiles during my exit interview with the management staff, my comment was met with an outbreak of hilarious laughter. Once the laughter died down, the GM asked me how I expected him to get his staff to work on "inclement weather days." That was a good question, because I had never experienced a blizzard. It was shortly after this visit that I experienced being "stranded" in my apartment by a blinding snow storm and then understood why a hotel would have snowmobiles as part of their capital equipment in a setting where severe winter weather was a normal occurrence.

After a few audits, things seemed to settle down and I probably learned more from the managers and employees on each of these hotel visits than I gave back in recommendations for improvements. However, the really good news was that there were no serious problems discovered on any of the visits. The company had the luxury of having a group of very seasoned, long-term GMs.

As I would learn later in my career, longevity and integrity are not always the hallmarks of every manager you will encounter in the hotel business or any other business. However, this company was blessed with many exceptional and dedicated managers. What can we learn from these audit experiences?

- Always be ready to accept new assignments as businesses, especially service businesses like hotels are dynamic. Be flexible and prepared to change as yesterday's plans may not be appropriate to meet the needs of tomorrow's guests.
- It is easy to sit in front of a computer and crunch numbers, but remember in the hotel business, the real action is where customers are being served. Take advantage of every opportunity on a daily basis to interact with as many employees and guests as possible.
- Pay attention to the differences in every setting in which you find yourself; grow personally, constantly adopting to new technologies and approaches to service delivery. You may encounter "snowmobiles" or some other seemingly strange assets or different procedures for getting the job done at any time. Get the facts and avoid jumping to conclusions about things that may seem to be unusual before reacting or commenting.
- Age and lack of experience need not be detriments to your success. Truly listen to and respect others and show them how your actions can contribute to their success, and lack of experience and age will become a non-issue. Always attempt to add value to the organization through your actions.

In the hotel business almost every day provides a new learning opportunity. As you will see in the next chapter, some of these learning opportunities can even turn out to be more fun than work!

7

Playing the Game

Everybody seems to like sports and keeping up with sporting events is an accepted part of the social side of any business environment, from "office pool" bets on everything from playoffs to championships to "Monday morning quarterbacking" discussions about weekend games to speculations about potential trades. However, no sport may be more important than golf, not even football. Talking about and playing golf seems to be a common topic in most business settings.

I had played a few rounds of golf with my cousin on the local pitch-and-putt course during high school, but to say I had developed any skill at the game of golf would be an exaggerated overstatement. Since my first day on the job was January 2nd, the subject of actually playing golf never came up until the snow started melting and the sun began to peek out from behind an endless sky of grey on a few tantalizing days.

Then, all of a sudden, spring was upon us, and the subject of golf was the major social topic of conversation during breaks, lunch and even after work as everyone was heading out the door. Almost everyone wanted to know my handicap. Not only did I not have a handicap, I had never even played on a regulation course! Nobody seemed to care; excuses for not playing were out of the question. No matter how much I persisted in saying that I did not know how to "play the game," Fred insisted that I join his foursome on their next outing.

To me, it was an offer that was too good to pass up and the other members of this foursome made the invitation that much more appealing, including the director of information technology at a local Fortune 500 plant and the plant manager from local food processing businesses. How could I turn down the opportunity to join these business people on their first day on the course?

I accepted the invitation, but there was a problem. I didn't own a set of clubs. After anguishing for way too long about whether to buy or borrow a set of clubs, Fred finally let me in on a little secret that everyone except me already knew. You can rent a set of clubs from the pro shop at the golf course. Realizing that I really was clueless about what to expect, Fred also filled me in on how to dress and what to expect on the golf course.

The big day came and I arrived ready to play. I had at least dressed appropriately and proceeded to rent my clubs, buy some balls and tees, and away we went for some practice on the putting green. On the first tee, after whiffing the ball, no pressure mind you, I finally dribbled the ball down the fairway. With this inauspicious start, the day should have gotten better but it didn't. After not having played for several years, my game got progressively worse. My golf skills were awful, but the camaraderie and conversations were exhilarating.

After the embarrassment of a less than stellar day, I was determined to do a much better job of "playing the game." So after a few lessons, and hitting countless buckets of balls at the driving range, I was ready to show my newly acquired skills. The next time I was invited to join a foursome, I was ready!

Golf ended up being a regular routine during the warm weather months. During the course of the summer, with a lot of practice and many invitations to join different foursomes, I became a little better than average at the game. So, other than having fun once I became comfortable with the game, what can we learn from gaining a little experience with developing what some would consider to be a leisure time skill?

- Golf is the game of the business world, so don't be surprised when the topic comes up and be prepared to enter the conversation with your own experiences.
- It's true what you hear; a lot of business is discussed while on the golf course. If you don't know how to play the game, take the time to learn or you will miss out on many important discussions.
- Pick up any book that covers the details of golf etiquette and brush up on the basics of the game before you hit the links. If you have never played the game, take some lessons and hit a few buckets of balls before you join your colleagues on the links. It is

extremely poor form and a lack of basic golf etiquette to hold up a foursome due to your lack of skills.
- If you want to be "in the know," learn to play the game and work at honing your skills. The game of golf proves that there is more to business than what you learn in the classroom or on-the-job and you can have some fun in the process!
- There will also be many other sporting opportunities that come along with working in the hotel business, many of these involving attending sporting events either because of the guests that stay in your property or the customers you serve.

Just when my game was improving, fall came and along with the change in seasons came another change in job duties. The current labor contract for the hotel was expiring and negotiations for a new contract appeared to be at a standstill. The potential impacts of a strike at the hotel were openly being discussed. As you will see in the next chapter, the events leading up to the strike and the actual strike were uncharted territory. These experiences would also prepare me for other challenges of working with organized labor later in my career.

8

The Strike

Growing up in a Southern right-to-work state (states having laws that prohibit requiring employees to join unions as a condition of obtaining or continuing employment), the only thing I knew about unions was what I had learned in college. I soon found out that sterile discussions and role-playing exercises about labor management relations that take place in a classroom were far removed from work place realities.

There had been talk around the office of the impending expiration of the hotel's current union contract and there had even been mention of a possible strike. Most of this was just talk, centered around stories from the old-timers about grievances, tensions, and personalities; and how they had shaped previous negotiations.

My first encounter with the tensions that began to rise during negotiations came with an invitation from the Vice President of Human Resources to join the contract negotiation process that was already in progress. As he explained my task, he said it would be a good learning experience and a good use of my financial skills. My task was to listen to all of the proposals presented by both sides during the negotiations, and then calculate their respective financial impacts on the hotel.

Listening to the proposals was fascinating. Sometimes these proposals and discussions were very civil, and at other times, they seemed to be downright hostile. The name calling, shouting, and four-letter words that came from both sides during these negotiation sessions were more common than expected.

As the name calling on the part of union leaders became more heated and there didn't seem like much movement on issues from either side, the reality of a strike was no longer a matter of speculation; it now seemed to be a real possibility. Union members had already voted to authorize a strike if their demands were not met and that threat was now creeping into almost every aspect of negotiations. Later, it was revealed to me that much of the shouting and bursts of temper were not unusual in open negotiations. These actions were just a form of "posturing" and served as an opportunity for participants to blow off some steam; but, at the time, it all seemed to be very serious.

After each of these formal negotiation sessions, I would present a financial analysis to the management team summarizing the costs or savings of everything that had been discussed. To my horror, after making one of these presentations, in my haste to complete this task, I discovered a mistake in my calculations. It wasn't just a minor mistake, it was a big one! One that could have cost the hotel almost $400,000 over the three-year life of the new contract.

I anguished over all of the bad things that might happen to me because of this mistake and what to do, and almost hesitated to admit it for fear of being fired. How could anyone forgive a mistake of this magnitude? After a restless night of tossing and turning with little sleep, I knew I had to "come clean" and admit my mistake.

The very first thing the next morning, I walked in to the Vice President of Human Resources' office, ready to face the consequences and laid out all the details. All he said was, "Everyone makes mistakes. Did you learn anything from your mistake?" That was it? What a relief, I wasn't going to be fired! With a huge sigh of relief, I said, "Yes, check and double-check all of your calculations no matter how pressed you are for time." After some more discussion about the issue, his final comment was, "We'll figure out how to correct the problem." He did figure out a way to correct the problem as negotiations continued over the next couple of days. This wasn't the last mistake I made, but it was certainly, to this day, the biggest!

Negotiations seemed to be grinding to a halt, and having never been through a strike, I was more than curious as to what would happen if a strike were called. Much to my surprise, I was informed that being classified as management (exempt from receiving overtime pay), I would be assigned to cover the duties of one or more hourly positions, if and when a strike occurred. For "safety reasons" and to meet guests' needs, I would be required to stay in the hotel and be expected to work what would amount to double-shifts throughout the strike. The word around the office was that, "guests' needs had to be met no matter what."

Along with the bad news that there would be a lot of extra work, there was also some good news! If the strike lasted more than a week, we would all get bonus pay for our extra work filling in for employees who had walked out in protest during the strike. As a fairly recent college graduate, the idea of bonus pay sent dollar signs dancing through my mind. I naively assumed (once again, that dangerous word), that with my education and experience, a cushy job on the front desk or night audit would be awaiting me.

Guess again, as a junior member of the management staff, I was informed that I would be assigned to work in the housekeeping department. There I would responsible for taking care of at least twenty rooms per day rather than the normal fifteen rooms. For me in this assignment , the only good news was that there would be no inspections of our work!

Negotiations continued almost non-stop leading up to the strike deadline. However, it was evident that the two sides were far apart, or that's the way it appeared from the animosity in the discussions. Sure enough, the deadline came without an agreement, and a strike was called. It was time to move into the hotel. Additional exempt classification employees had also been brought in to "beef-up" staffing from other properties. Some of these people I had already met on internal audit assignments.

* * *

My first full day as a housekeeper was awkward and slow, but the guests were understanding, especially those that were the last on the list. It was close to 8:00 p.m. before I got around to cleaning up the last room. By the time the last pillow was tucked into its pillow case and the final bedspread was neatly smoothed, I was exhausted and ready to crash. What had started out as an adrenaline-filled 8:00 a.m. morning ended with an exhausted flop into bed in the last room on my list, number 641, mine.

The following day was more of the same, just one room after another. The third day was just like the first and the second days, except that now I was now beginning to get into the rhythm of the job. Maybe the rooms weren't quite as clean, but the last room was finished and the housekeeping cart was back in the closet by 6:00 p.m., stocked and ready to go for the next day. This seemed like a small victory. However, I still wonder to this day if anyone noticed my vacuuming or the lack thereof.

After a good night's sleep and sharing some great stories and feeling a sense of comradeship with my fellow "workers" in the break room, I was ready to do it all again. The thought of a bonus check in the not too distant future was more than enough motivation to make cleaning twenty rooms each day seem like a doable task.

Then, poof! My dreams of a bonus check were shattered at breakfast the next morning. It was announced that a settlement had been reached and the strike had been called off. Suddenly all of the drama was over as the two sides had come to an agreement and it was time to get back to our normal job duties. The strike had lasted less than a week, so the past three days had turned into just another "learning experience."

After things got back to normal, it was revealed that the stumbling block in the negotiations had been wages for the bartenders, the smallest and most vocal bargaining unit in the union. What was the wage difference between the two sides that had resulted in the three-day strike? Twenty cents an hour!

Once again, the events in this episode provide a number of learning opportunities. Think about all that happened and realize that:

- College doesn't preclude you from making, or more importantly, taking responsibility for making mistakes. A mistake in a classroom, a test, or on a paper can be the difference between an A, B, or even a C. So, you quickly learn to fear mistakes. In contrast, many successful business people will tell you that they have made many mistakes.
- When you make mistakes, don't try to cover them up. Quickly admit them so remediation can begin immediately. Attempting to hide a mistake or pretending like it didn't happen is the same as lying; all it will do is make your problem worse.
- Conflict often involves posturing and, at times, the audible sounds of disagreement don't reveal the true emotions or intentions of the parties.

- Politics play an important part of every organization, including unions.
- Strikes tend to be either very short, three days or less, or much longer, often lasting several weeks. Many times after long and contentious negotiations, strikes are called to "let off steam," a time when union members can walk the picket line and rant at management while at the same time management is forced to perform the tasks of those on strike. If a strike lasts more than a few days, there are usually serious issues because union members seldom want to live on what little they can make from strike pay. Our strike was just one of those "garden variety strikes" designed to let off a little steam.

After weeks of negotiations and the strike, things quickly settled down to normal routines with the exception of a "little problem" in one of the hotel's food and beverage outlets. As you will see in the next chapter, coming off of a strike may not have been the best time to delve into this problem, but problems rarely present themselves at convenient times.

9

The Spy

What started out as a simple special assignment after "The Strike" soon turned into anything but simple. Liquor costs in the formal dining room had been creeping up over the past few months; starting from an average of about 29% and growing to a whopping 36% in just a few short months. Stated as a percentage, this is a big increase, but when these percentages are translated into dollars they had a big impact on the bottom line (or, stated another way, a lot less profit) for the hotel. In addition, to typical beer and spirit sales, the restaurant served many high-end guests which resulted in a robust wine business. Costs definitely appeared to have gotten out of hand and something had to be done, but what?

Fred explained the problem and asked me to do some investigating. The first step, Plan A, was simple. Go back through the liquor invoices for the past six months and see if there had been any increases in quantities ordered or in our wholesale costs from suppliers. This was a simple plan as it only involved following a paper trail and some number crunching. First, changes in order quantities could signal the possibility of "leakage," which would require further investigation. Second, if there had been any cost increases that had slipped through the system, the solution would be fairly simple; raise prices to reflect the increased costs on the next reprinting of the menus. However, as simple as that may sound, it might not work, as the restaurant's menu prices were already at the top end of the market.

After this initial investigation turned up nothing out of the ordinary, it was time to move on to Plan B. Following a brief discussion with the VP of Food and Beverage, Plan B was initiated. The idea behind Plan B was to reconcile the amount of liquor that was being sold based on cash register receipts against the amount of inventory usage. In most restaurant settings, this would have also been simple, as inventory and pouring amounts are computer controlled. However, in this restaurant, the free-pour system was still being used.

As Plan B was initiated, the VP of Food and Beverage had already talked with the operations managers and decided that I would join the head bartender when he took his nightly inventory and prepared his requisition to replenish the bar stock for the next day. Since he was scheduled to work from 4:00 p.m. to 11:00 p.m., and not wanting to spend any more time than necessary on this task, I suggested, that if possible, we take the inventory at the beginning of his shift the next day. We all agreed, and took inventory and he completed the requisition form at the beginning of the shift. Everything appeared to be in order.

After two weeks of going through this process, there was still no change in costs. As a continuation and modification of Plan

B, Fred, along with the VP of Food and Beverage and his operations management team, had decided that I should shadow the head bartender as he performed his routines and take inventory at the end of the shift. This meant that I got to do my regular office tasks from 8:00 a.m. to 5:00 p.m. and then come back for another hour or two late in the evening to shadow the inventory and requisition process. One side benefit was that I got to stay in the hotel and my evening meal was "comp'ed."

Even with this change, the results were still the same; costs did not drop to normal levels. In addition, if you think about it, I am so lucky I didn't get a grievance filed against me, because as you may remember, it was the bartenders who had been problematic during the union negotiations leading up to "The Strike."

Let's review how things were going. Both Plan A and Plan B yielded no solutions. Before you think that a lot of effort was being put into what seemed like a puny problem, you need to know that the costs of liquor sales for this restaurant amounted to over $30,000 a week. So, a 7% increase in costs easily surpassed $2,000 in higher expenses each month. Another way to think about this problem would be to consider the fact that if the cost problem could be solved, there was the potential for almost $100,000 in additional profit each year from just this one beverage venue.

The failure of both Plans A and B puzzled all of us. One of these plans should have provided an easy answer to our problem unless, as some assumed, we were experiencing dishonesty on the part of the bartending staff. Could they be pouring drinks without "ringing them up?" Could they just be over-pouring or refilling customers' glasses without charging them in an attempt to garner larger tips? The questions were many, but the answers continued to be elusive.

Based on these questions and a lack of answers, Fred and the VP of Food and Beverage decided to implement what became known as Plan C. Before describing Plan C, you need to remember how well the GMs received me when I arrived for the internal audits. Well, the unionized bartenders and especially the head bartender were even less enthusiastic when they learned that I would be present during their entire shift.

Plan C required that I sit at the bar between 4:00 p.m. and 11:00 p.m. and observe everything the bartenders did. It was a busy bar, so there was little chance for boredom and not much conversation with the bartenders who seemed to be in constant motion. I did have some interesting conversations with the guests and learned how to appear to be drinking and enjoy myself without getting buzzed.

Most hotel companies have policies against consuming alcoholic beverages while working, so you may want to consider this tactic. If you order a gin and tonic with a slice of lime but without the gin, it looks like you are having an alcoholic beverage when in fact, you are not. This is a trick I employed many times in situations where people were imbibing and I wanted to fit in but still keep my wits about me.

The actions in Plan C were designed to last for a week, Monday through Sunday. On the first two days of the assignment, the bartenders basically ignored me, except when I asked a question. In fact "ignored," is an understatement, they shunned me. The head bartender even called me "a spy."

He was right, but the label still stung. By the third day, the ice had begun to break. I had become a fixture and even got a little recognition as I took my usual seat at the end of the bar where I could watch the cash register and all of their mixing gyrations and "pourings." After a week, all I learned was that the bartenders were very busy, professional, and competent. I only observed one significant inconsistency in all of those hours. One bartender rang up a beer, but served a mixed drink. As busy as the bar was that evening, it was probably just a mistake.

What was being done about completing my other financial work in the accounting office? While I was off on this espionage assignment, as expected, I did the critical parts of that too, but with shortened hours.

Even with all of the time and effort expended with Plans A, B, and C, the mystery of why the costs were out of line was never solved. Over time, costs gradually came down, but, not to the targeted cost range. Reflecting back on these events, I still wonder if the answer might have been found in bartender dishonesty that could have been uncovered with more investigation, or if it had something to do with wine sales.

For some reason, at the time, none of us ever thought to look into wine inventory or wine sales. Since it was a high-end, gourmet restaurant, we did sell a significant amount of wine. In hindsight, after a cooling off period, perhaps management should have continued the investigation much more discreetly. I was an obvious spy inserted by management, so any dishonest person (e.g. bartenders) knew to be on the lookout for me and what I could observe. An alternative would have been to arrange for someone else, a "mystery shopper," who could blend in and make observations that might have been kept secret from me.

Maybe the mystery could have been solved with Plan D, but satisfied that no more investigating or "spying" was in order, everyone's attention had shifted and moved on to other operational issues. Even though this had not been an enjoyable task for either me or the bartenders, there was much to be learned from this assignment.

- The hotel business is dynamic. One of the things that you quickly learn in the hotel business is that there are a lot of moving parts to a successful operation and when you solve one problem, there will surely be another problem that pops up to command your attention.
- Sometimes problems are small and simple and sometimes they are big and complex. Whether they are big or small, all problems are worth investigating and solving. And, upon investigation, what may first appear to be only a small problem may, in fact, just be the tip of an iceberg of a much bigger problem.
- Successful hotel operations require paying constant attention to details. The good news is, if you pay attention to and take care of the details, the details will often take care of themselves. As was true in this

case, at least in the short run, not every problem will be solvable, but problem investigation is an important part of paying attention to details.
- Policies such as those prohibiting the consumption of alcoholic beverages on the job are meant for the good of the employees and to protect the hotel. Respect those policies and learn how to operate within their constraints.
- Mystery shoppers can provide valuable insights into both customer service and operational issues.

Not finding a solution to this problem was disappointing; but the daily business of the hotel marched on and guests continued to arrive and needed to be served. That's what the business is all about, customer service! However, as the next chapter illustrates, sometimes decision making can defy logic.

10

"You Just Don't Understand"

This was a really big assignment, one where I could use everything I learned in my finance classes. It would be a great opportunity to showcase my talents! The corporation had been approached about the possibility of purchasing a medium-sized resort hotel in a beautiful sub-tropical setting. The office was buzzing about the opportunity, especially the possibility of being sent there on assignment in the winter.

It seemed like everyone in the corporate office from the executive suite to the support staff was interested in purchasing this hotel. The corporation was just beginning to penetrate the Southern States, and this particular opportunity fit with the desire to purchase or build more hotels in the Sunbelt. Although the assignment had been given to me by the Controller, I was told that the President and the V. P. of Operations were both very interested and would be "keeping close tabs" on my progress.

They were indeed interested; and they not only asked a lot of questions as I was putting together my analysis, but they also provided a lot of input as I searched for data on comparable operations and tried to extrapolate potential trends on performance metrics from our current operations. Piecing together all of the needed financial information was no easy task. Complicating the analysis was the fact that the property was old and in need of extensive renovations to meet our desired image. As was customary with any type of analysis like this, three potential estimates were requested: optimistic, most likely, and pessimistic.

My task was to determine if it made sense to make a multi-million dollar investment. I threw myself into this assignment working late into the evening and coming in on weekends to be in the office when there would be limited interruptions. I analyzed everything from the expected payback period to net present value. There wasn't a day that went by that one of the executives who was involved in some way in this potential acquisition didn't stop by to ask me how the work was progressing.

Even with all of the positive energy that was surrounding this potential acquisition, the further I got into my analysis, the more troubled I became. No matter how I crunched the numbers, the investment just would not seem to be profitable. It would have been easy to just say that the purchase, "wouldn't pencil out," except for the fact that all of the executives seemed to be already "packing their bags" to check out their planned purchase. The outcome of my analysis appeared to be the only thing holding them back. It had been a long hard winter with a lot of snow and very little sunshine, so the thought of a warm winter location with tropical breezes probably seemed even more enticing than usual. But no matter how hard I tried to project a positive financial future for the property, I just couldn't arrive at a positive outcome.

Two weeks into my analysis, the now constant anguishing over what to do, suddenly came to a rapid halt. The V. P. of Operations asked me to come to his office and share my findings. After about fifteen minutes of explaining why the purchase didn't make any financial sense, he made a statement that has always haunted me. It went something like this, "You just don't understand; we want to own that property. You go back and rework your numbers until this purchase makes sense."

With that said, the meeting was over. Fred, in his usual low-key mentoring fashion, later revealed that the executive team really wanted this property because of its location. They already had been planning for several corporate meetings at the new property.

My dilemma now shifted – should I stand by my painstakingly prepared analysis or massage the numbers to make the transaction look financially viable? Maybe I was just not seeing the "big picture." I'll let you think about how you might answer that question before telling you what I did.

It didn't take me long to make my decision. Maybe my assumptions (there's that word again) were wrong. Maybe projected occupancy figures were too conservative. After renovations were completed, maybe food and beverage revenues might surprise us on the upside. Maybe we could attract more convention and meeting business than was being built into the projections. Maybe we could spend less on renovations. Maybe I just needed to change my assumptions. Whatever the possibilities, I went back and diligently revisited my analyses and found a way to make the purchase marginally make sense.

In hindsight, I'm not sure management really needed my analyses other than to justify a purchase decision that seemed to have already been made. It wasn't as if upper management needed my permission to buy the property or couldn't override my recommendation. However, more than I realized at the time, being new to the job and wanting to please my superiors, I was allowing myself to be pressured. Being pressured into making a recommendation where I had some lingering doubts felt uncomfortable, but it was not career threatening.

From a financial perspective the property was never a big success. At least it always achieved break even or, in some years, made a little money. From a marketing perspective, the property was an eye-catching showcase after the remodel. There was finally a high-quality resort style Sunbelt property in the corporation's portfolio.

So, what lessons can be learned from this experience?

- Know what the ultimate goal is; it can save you a lot of time and frustration. Ask a lot of questions and listen closely to discern both what is being said and what is being left unsaid, but is clearly desired.

- Numbers don't lie, but if you massage them long enough, they often will produce whatever answer the manipulator desires.
- Don't jump to conclusions. Individual goals, especially those of top-level executives, may transcend logic from your perspective, even seeming to out-weigh your view of common sense. However, what may seem to be common sense in your world and at your level of understanding may not reflect long-term strategic objectives.
- Stay firm to your convictions. Don't be swayed by what your superiors tell you to do when you don't agree. If you disagree with a course of action, or a decision, go on record and say so.
- Numbers and analytical analysis are not the end-all and be-all for decision making. They are just part of the process and a piece of the puzzle.

In a way, I was glad the purchase decision was made, as I had several opportunities to visit and work with the staff in this property. There will be more on that later, but as I would soon learn, my mentors had some big plans for me in the immediate future.

11

Decision Time

At this early stage in my career, the excitement of hotel operations was definitely getting into my blood. I began looking forward to heading out on the road, meeting a whole new group of people, and participating in new "learning experiences" even when, at times, I was still greeted with the moniker, "snoop."

My enthusiasm must have shown a little too much as Fred said that he had volunteered me for a three-week assignment, if I didn't object. I'm not sure if objecting was ever an option, so the answer was yes, even before I knew anything about the assignment. This type of volunteering behavior without asking a lot of questions would manifest itself again in the future, but more about that later.

In this new assignment, I was to be put out "on loan" to one of the smaller properties in the chain for three weeks. I would work with, "shadow (follow and observe)" the Assistant General Manager for one week and then take over some of his duties for two weeks while the GM was on vacation.

This time the GM welcomed my arrival. This was an especially busy 110-room suburban property that ran an annual occupancy rate of just over 90% and a full-service dining room that often had a line of people waiting for a table. The hotel also had a very active catering department that served the needs of many social functions and local service organizations, so the hotel was always filled with activity. The property was not only well-run, it was also a money-maker for the corporation. One other thing quickly became evident at this hotel. Although everyone in management dressed formally, they interacted with each other informally. First names were the order of business and this took some getting used to.

The assignment was for the last three weeks of June, a time that the GM would not typically take a vacation, but it was a special occasion. Anyway, there really wasn't a good time for the GM to take a vacation, as this property was always busy. But, everyone had confidence in this GM's decision to take some time off. Besides, he was taking the time off for the final preparations for his wedding and honeymoon. Since he had been in charge of this property for all twenty years of its existence and his assistant had been with him for fifteen years, and his administrative assistant had been at the property for fourteen years, there was no question that the property would be in good hands.

They made a good team, and everyone in the corporate office knew it. High occupancy, an impeccable record of positive customer comments, and a solid track record of profitability were hallmarks of this well-run operation. The risk factors for the corporate office of sending me in to assist were minimal and I was told before leaving by several people, I would get to witness some best practices while lending a hand.

The Assistant GM, I soon learned, had no desire to move on to another location and was content to remain in his second-in-command position until the GM retired. Being a GM in a successful property in his hometown was his career aspiration.

Three weeks turned out to be too short of a time period to learn everything there was to absorb from working in this "well-oiled" machine. There was very little turnover among the staff, everyone knew their jobs, and the focus in completing their tasks always seemed to be on satisfying the guests. All I had to do was to get up each morning and walk downstairs and start a new day by blending in, observing, and helping out whenever needed.

I did get picked on about my age, but the most teasing I got was about my accent. Being in a northern property my Texas drawl was an oddity. After a couple of days of teasing, I decided to do everything possible to get rid of the accent. It didn't take long, and with a conscious effort on my part, it was starting to disappear by the end of my stay. I had stopped using words like "ya'll" and "fixin' to." Ditching the accent and taking on a "radio announcer's" voice were an added bonus as it helped me in my career when dealing with people from different parts of the country. Most people could never guess where I was originally from.

It wasn't long into this assignment until it became apparent that the only reason I was there was that the GM always wanted "someone in charge" at all times on the property. My presence may have eased his mind, but as green as I was, I'm not sure what I would have done if there had been a crucial decision, other than call the Assistant GM.

Coming back to the accounting office after this assignment made the routine of my day-to-day activities seem bland. By the way, have I mentioned that by now I was thoroughly hooked on the hotel business? To put it mildly, the hotel business is intoxicating! I was definitely looking forward to more opportunities to learn.

My restlessness must have showed, as Fred stopped by my desk one day and said, "Let's go see the V. P. of Operations." With my coat always on now, we strode out together and down the hall for a predestined meeting.

The choices presented in this meeting were simple. The first choice; I could stay in the corporate office and continue to work on my usual tasks and other special assignments. This choice; however, came with a caveat. I should plan on going back to school part-time with the goal of completing the necessary course work to become a Certified Public Accountant (CPA). As it was gently put to me, advancement opportunities in the corporate office would be limited without the CPA designation. The second choice; take a hotel operations position in the field.

As you will see later on, I have a tendency to have trouble making up my mind. However in this situation, it didn't take long to think about these two choices. The active lifestyle of hotel operations as opposed to the thought of a career of "number crunching" made my decision a "no-brainer." In fact,

An Accidental Hotelier

I only had one question, before making a final commitment. "Could the position be in one of the Southern properties?" Growing up in warm country where bitter cold and snow were novelties, I had seen enough blizzards and sub-zero overcast days, and was ready to be warm again! When they said yes, I said yes, not even asking what the assignment would be or where it would be.

One month after that eventful meeting, another meeting was arranged to meet my new boss, pending his approval. He was the newly appointed GM of a very large center convention hotel that was six months away from completion, and it was being constructed in the South. And, what would be my assignment? If he agreed that I was the right person to join his staff, I would be in charge of setting up and running the accounting and human resources office. That MBA might come in handy some day, but it seemed far away now, and the only thing I knew for certain was that I was officially on the path to becoming a hotelier!

The lessons from these experiences are numerous:

- The hotel business is an exciting business that can easily become addictive. No day is ever the same and you are constantly on the move working with employees and serving guests.
- Always be flexible and adapt to new situations. Don't be afraid to volunteer for new assignments. There is always something new to learn. Once again, learn the culture in which you will be working and adapt to fit in.
- Experience is a wonderful teacher and learning from the best can provide a wealth of knowledge for later

application. Although classroom knowledge creates a solid foundation for career entry and growth, there is so much more to be learned from practical on-the-job experiences.
- Don't stay in a job just for the paycheck. Follow your passions! When you enjoy your job, it no longer seems like work!

The realities of my new career path were beginning to set in. But, before I could move on to my next assignment, there was still some very important work to be done in my current position, so let's move on to the next chapter and another learning experience.

12

Words of Wisdom

If you didn't already know it, there are two primary goals in the hotel business. The first is to get "as many heads in beds as possible" or, stated another way, "to achieve the highest possible level of occupancy." The second goal is to obtain the maximum amount of revenue as possible. So, when you pay the "rack rate" for your stay in a lodging property, you have contributed to both goals. From a technical perspective, when you combine both of these goals you are practicing revenue management or, as it is still sometimes called, yield management.

The other thing you may already know is that the rooms side of the hotel business carries a much higher profit margin than the food and beverage side of the business. In addition, there are far fewer problems to deal with in the rooms side as opposed to the food and beverage side of the business. Rooms and food and beverage comprise the basics of the operational and financial components of the hotel business. But, there is more to the hotel business than just generating revenues; there is also the important people side of the business.

The people side of the business, both employees and guests, will always be a challenge from a managerial and customer relations perspective, but this side of the business also holds the possibility of some potentially serious interpersonal problems. When you combine rooms with alcoholic beverages, you encounter the age-old dilemma in the hotel business of, "beds and booze." Just let your imagination run for a moment and you should be able to quickly conjure up a few "X-rated images" as well as other potential sexual harassment situations.

The combination of "beds and booze" with employees who work closely together for long hours and guests who are often looking for a "good time" while away from home, has been the undoing of many a hotelier's career who has let his/her guard down in a moment of indiscretion. While working in the corporate office, these temptations had never really been an issue, because I was just working in an office and not a hotel. However, with my new assignment at the property level, it would be a different story! So, before leaving to assume these new duties, I got the "beds and booze" lecture from not one, but two, corporate executives.

The, "words of wisdom" lectures from both of these executives was that the temptations will always be persistent, but to succumb to them would be a career stopper. As you will see in events that unfold in later chapters, the hotel business can be "very sexy if not seductive" as you find yourself dealing with a lot of glamorous people in a fun-filled atmosphere. In this type of setting, it could be easy to get caught up in the moment.

The lessons to be learned from this short incident are succinct, but profound.

- Don't forget that you are in fact, in the people business! As part of this business, there are two primary goals, achieving maximum occupancy and maximizing revenue from that occupancy. To achieve these goals requires attracting guests and motivating employees to serve these guests so that they will become repeat customers. You are on stage every day, and every action you take is being observed and critiqued by both employees and guests.
- Enjoy interacting with and being around your co-workers and guests, but check your hormones at the door when you go to work. Life is too short to sacrifice your career to temptation.
- Many hotel companies have human resource policies that prohibit employees from enjoying the 'night life" and imbibing while either on- or off-duty on hotel property, and for good reason. There are just too many temptations and alcohol will impair your judgment.
- Read and specifically follow all sexual harassment policies. Behaving morally and ethically isn't all that complicated if you remember to think about what the newspaper or social media banners the next day might say about your actions. If the lead for the story would embarrass you or those whose opinions you value, just don't do it!

Having been armed with these "words of wisdom" and a few other sage comments from mentors, superiors and colleagues, it was off to new adventures. As you will see in the next chapter, the hotel business is filled with time-honored traditions that date back from the time when innkeepers said, "come in, be my guest."

14

Traditions

You may have noticed that there is no Chapter 13 in this book. The fact that there is no Chapter 13, is not a mistake or oversight. As you will see in this incident, there are many important traditions in the hotel business.

When I arrived at my new assignment, the hotel was well under construction as concrete for the top floor was being poured. Construction was proceeding according to plan, and, even though the scheduled opening for the hotel was still several months away, all eyes were already being focused on plans for the grand opening. Shortly after arriving, I got to witness the first of a litany of many time-honored traditions that take place in the construction and opening of a new hotel.

The final pour of concrete for the roof was just being completed. When this task was completed, a small evergreen tree was placed on the roof. This symbolic gesture was made to show that the building would always be firmly rooted to the ground from that day forward. This property would "officially" be a fourteen story hotel. In reality it was only a thirteen story hotel, but if you have ever looked at the buttons on the elevator key pad of a hotel, you will notice another hotel tradition. There are no thirteenth floors.

Hoteliers long ago discovered that many guests are superstitious and have no desire to stay on the thirteenth floor of a hotel. Skipping from the twelfth to the fourteenth floor is just one more time-honored hotel tradition. The same is true for hotel room numbers, you will have to search for a long time to find a room number ending in the number thirteen. Now you can see why there is no Chapter 13 in a book about becoming a hotelier!

Although the hotel hadn't been planned with a large number of rooms, the building site provided an opportunity to create an impressive ballroom and numerous medium-sized meeting rooms. When construction was completed, this would be one of the newest downtown convention hotels in the state, and its opening was eagerly anticipated.

As the opening date approached, another hotel tradition, a grand opening, was being planned to announce the fact that a hotel was open for business. Invitation lists were being drawn up and personal calls were being made to insure that the who's who of business, government, and society would be on hand for the grand opening ceremonies and events.

During the final weeks before the grand opening, the usual construction snags and delays in deliveries of furniture, fixtures, and equipment were experienced. This is not uncommon for any large construction project, and especially not for any construction and furnishing project as complex as a hotel.

Problems were encountered, but solutions to these problems were quickly found because everyone, no matter what their position, pitched in to make the scheduled opening day a reality. When you are part of an opening team for a hotel, job descriptions and titles don't mean much. Work days get longer and everyone focuses all of their attention on making the opening a reality.

As contractor punch lists were approved, and safety measures were double-checked, non-construction employees were allowed to enter portions of the property. The GM, sales staff, and key members of the food and beverage department began moving from off-site office space into their new main floor offices in the unfinished hotel.

Hard hats were still required, but tours to show off the grandeur and potential of the meeting spaces were now possible. Next, it was my turn to start moving in, as the accounting and human resources office space was soon completed. Plans could now be implemented for equipping all of the office space, staffing the hotel, and orienting and training the new recruits we were bringing on-board.

It didn't take long to get our supporting staff office space up and running. With the help of the GM, we quickly hired a Receptionist/Human Resources Clerk, an Assistant Controller, and a Purchasing Agent. Hiring an Accounts Payable Clerk and an Accounts Receivable Clerk filled out our staffing complement. Being fully staffed, I then split my time between getting our office organized and the staff trained and helping out with solving opening details along with all the other members of the management staff.

The week before the targeted "soft opening" was chaotic, with everyone on the management staff putting in twelve to fifteen hour work days, taking care of what seemed to be an unending list of details in need of attention. Finally, and with no fan-fare we had reached that critical stage in the construction of every hotel project -- the "soft opening."

When the construction barricades and fencing was cleared away from the main entrance, curiosity seekers and a few prospective guests ventured in the front doors and asked, "If we were open for business." This "soft opening" period is a time when a hotel is not officially open for business, but is ready to handle a few invited (mostly hotel employees) as well as some walk-in guests to "check in" in order to break in the staff and test out the systems and procedures. The "soft opening" phase was compressed into a short two week period, as grand opening ceremonies and events had already been scheduled.

As construction debris disappeared and the sounds of vacuum cleaners replaced that of saws and hammers, we were finally ready to officially welcome a few guests. Even with the understanding that there would be some construction noise and that the restaurant would not be open, we still got a few takers with our "teaser" rates. With positive comments from our paying guests about the luxury of our rooms and the friendliness of our staff, plus the experiences of several of us who just "crashed" in guest rooms at the end of long days, it appeared as if all systems were go and we were finally ready to open the doors. The hotel had been under construction for almost two years, and we were all looking forward to the prospects of generating some revenues and getting into the routine of serving guests; after all, there had been months and months of expenses and no revenues.

The big day finally arrived! Our corporate executives, reporters, photographers, politicians, business people, and other local dignitaries gathered for the official ribbon-cutting ceremony. There was no question in anybody's mind that it was "show time!"

As part of the opening ceremonies, yet another hotel tradition is performed. The key to the front door of the hotel was symbolically tossed onto the roof. This simple gesture, as well as the placing of the evergreen tree on the top of the building when the roof is completed, brings the deeply seated traditions in hotel lore full circle. For, when the key is tossed on the roof, it is a symbol that the doors of the hotel will always be open and the staff will be ready to serve weary travelers; twenty-four hours a day, seven days a week.

FYI

You can't talk about hotel traditions without saying something about the pineapple. Legend has it that New England sea captains returning from a voyage back to the colonies through the

Caribbean Islands would spear a pineapple on the fence post in front of their homes to let it be known that it had been a safe voyage and all were welcome. The pineapple has since become a welcome symbol and a sign of hospitality.

Reservations were now being taken on a daily basis and guests were beginning to trickle in. The fact that guests did not flood in, was a good thing as each day revealed operational kinks and small problems that still needed to be solved. But, after several days of getting used to working with each other and becoming familiar with the nuances of our operating systems, everyone began settling into their routines. Now that we were in business, we all began to eagerly anticipate the final hotel tradition -- grand opening festivities.

There is much to be learned from traditions.

- Specific, clearly communicated and meaningful goals with which everyone can identify, like opening a new hotel, always seem to bring out the best in people. They can focus their time and energy on tangible accomplishments that are part of making a dream become a reality.
- There are many formalities and time-honored traditions that are ritualistically observed in the hotel business. Each of these traditions carries a very special

meaning and they have all become part of the lore of the hotel business and are practiced with recognition and often accompanied with a great deal of "fan-fare."

- The evergreen tree being placed on the roof as construction is topped-off signifies not only longevity, but also permanence as the building becomes firmly rooted in the ground.
- The absence of a thirteenth floor and room numbers ending in thirteen shows deference to guests who might hold deep superstitions about this "unlucky" number.
- The key being tossed on the roof as the doors to the hotel are officially opened during the ribbon cutting ceremony signifies that no matter what happens in the world, shelter will always be available for the weary traveler.
- The grand opening ceremonies provide an opportunity to showcase everything a new property has to offer the host community and future guests. It is your house and you are part of the team that makes "the house work." Showcasing pride in "ownership" creates the foundation for continuing success.

While traditions bring with them a sense of continuity, purpose, pride, and connectivity; sometimes things don't always go as planned. As you will see in the next chapter, when an "unwelcomed guest" arrives, plans for a perfect evening must be changed.

15

A Grand Opening Surprise

The last of the great hotel traditions had finally arrived, and on the eve of the grand opening, every square foot of the hotel's massive banquet and meeting room space was decked out for the festivities with bountiful bouquets of flowers. In addition, a whole forest of greenery had been brought in as all of the public areas on the property had been staged to create a spectacular setting. The big day had finally arrived; planning was over and it was "show time!"

On the evening of the grand opening, a steady stream of guests arrived in their tuxedos and evening gowns and began mixing and mingling while sampling hors-d'oeuvres, sipping champagne, and listening to the melodious tunes of a string quartette and grand piano. The evening was off to a spectacular start. After short welcoming speeches from the President of the corporation and the GM, guided tours to showcase all of the features and amenities of this magnificent new property began. The champagne was flowing freely as the mixing, mingling, eating, and drinking continued.

An Accidental Hotelier

By the sounds of conversations, laughter, and the "ooh's and aah's" that came from our guests as they were enjoying the lavish spread of hors d'oeuvres and tours; the grand opening was a success. No surprises so far, everything was going as planned. Then all of a sudden, it happened!

I was standing at the bottom of an expansive spiral staircase that led from the upper level registration lobby of the hotel down to the lower level banquet and meeting areas where we were checking the engraved invitations to the event and admitting guests to the festivities. The staircase leading down to the lower level curved around a 20-foot-long transecting chandelier that appeared as if it were magically suspended from the ceiling and stopped just eight feet above a large reflecting pool with a bubbling fountain at the base of the staircase.

The setting was almost surreal. Twinkling lights had been added around the fountain for the festivities, the water was gurgling, soft music wafted through the air, and the buzz of pleasant conversations could be heard everywhere. There I was at the base of the staircase, visiting with an attractive young lady (this guest would later become my wife) when, all of a sudden, the voice of a man belting out a Tarzan scream shattered this bucolic scene.

As I looked up, to my horror, the man belting out the scream jumped out from the rail at the top of the staircase, and grabbed the middle of the chandelier that was a good eight feet in front of him in a bear hug. Each of the dozens of smaller light fixtures that protruded from the main column of the chandelier might have resembled rungs on a ladder, but they were not designed to be load-bearing and proved to be no match for his weight.

The end result of his theatrics -- our would-be Tarzan's decent down the chandelier proceeded unimpeded with a splash into the reflecting pool. In retrospect, it all seemed to unfold in slow motion, but it only took a few seconds for everything to happen. There was only the sickening rapid-fire clink, clink, clink, clink as each of the chandelier's extensions methodically broke off with his decent. The next thing we knew, Tarzan had come to the end of the chandelier and hit one of the fountain fixtures in the reflecting pool. He landed on his back with one of the fountain fixtures impaling his back and puncturing his spleen.

The Food and Beverage Director who seemed to just appear from nowhere helped me get the man out of the fountain and one of the off-duty police officers who had been hired as security for the event called in the paramedics. You're always told to never move anyone who may have suffered a back injury, but common sense and adrenaline and the specter of a drowning man overrode basic safety training and probably saved the man's life. Although it was probably only a few minutes before the ambulance arrived, it seemed like an eternity.

Tarzan's girlfriend was in hysterics, and a crowd had gathered around. Luckily the paramedics whisked Tarzan off to the emergency room and things quickly settled back to normal. Normal, that is, after the Food and Beverage Director found a large bottle of blue food coloring in the kitchen and poured it into the reflecting pool to conceal the blood-stained water.

How can I remember all of these details? The answer is simple. Through training, I was always taught to debrief with everyone involved in an incident and document significant events. At the end of the evening I took the time to write down as many of the details as I could remember. This was a good thing, as the hotel was sued and I, along with other witnesses were deposed. Why was the hotel sued? Believe it or not, this "unwelcomed guest" claimed that when he saw our chandelier, he just couldn't help but leap out and try to swing on it to impress his girlfriend.

Without a doubt, this was an unforgettable Grand Opening! The hotel business can be both deceptively routine and yet dynamic; hours and hours of the same and then moments of sheer excitement and sometimes terror. Other than learning to expect the unexpected and being able to roll with the punches, what can we learn from these experiences?

- There are many, many glamorous moments in the hotel business and many interesting people who will cross you path on a regular basis. Enjoy each of these signature moments!
- People can be unpredictable, so be flexible and expect the unexpected. No matter how well you plan, how well you design your systems and procedures, and how well you train your employees' know that there will sometimes be circumstances and events that cannot be anticipated and require you to change those plans.
- Surprises, both good and bad, will always happen especially when you least expect them, so be prepared

for the unexpected! Prepare as many contingency plans as possible to deal with the unexpected.
- Document, document, document! Whenever you are faced with an event involving people that could even have the slightest possibility of leading to any type of legal action, take notes. Write down everything about the event that you can remember immediately, so you never have to rely on your memory.

With the Grand Opening behind us, it was time to settle into the routine of daily operations. Routines should be simple; but maybe not, if you get too deep into micro-managing the details of those daily operations as the next incident proves.

16

When in Doubt, Call!

The night audit is a routine that requires a great deal of attention to detail. The night audit is performed by individuals that enjoy detail work and can handle working in the solitude that comes with the graveyard shift from 11:00 p.m. to 7:00 a.m.

In addition to general guest services, they serve as front desk clerks (guest services' agents), cashiers and perform the night auditor bookkeeping functions that must be completed at the end of each day. They also have to make some judgment calls when reservations have not been guaranteed with a credit card and guests who do not show up. Should they take a risk and rent to generate maximum revenue and risk "walking" a guest when the house is full, or just play it safe and leave the room empty?

Dependable night auditors with a customer service attitude are hard to find and just as hard to keep. Night auditors reconcile all of the day's transactions to make sure that revenue has been recorded properly for every sales transaction. Like many other tasks in the hotel business, the night audit recurred every day.

We had been lucky in finding two full-time and one part-time night auditors. They were all very good at performing the night auditor bookkeeping functions. They had not only proven to be dependable (a particularly important trait in this position), but they were also very service oriented; in short, they were a blessing.

FYI

Revenue management is the art and science of generating the highest possible levels of occupancy and revenue or yield each and every day. The algorithms built into computer programs that set room rates for each category for days, weeks, months and even years in advance are impressive and change by the hour and even minute. But, what happens when a guest who has reserved a room for two nights decides to stay four nights and the hotel is already sold out? If you are working on the front desk, you don't control the computer, so chances are you will not be able to honor an incoming reservation and will have to "walk" a guest. Even though you can arrange to send this "walked" guest to another hotel, pay for the room and the cab, prepare to be verbally abused. The first few times this happens, it will be painful, but "time heals all wounds" and you will soon learn to deal with this and other problems that technology throws your way.

Although in a large hotel, there can be tens of thousands of dollars of daily sales transactions, the process of reconciliation is usually fairly straight forward. Even in a very busy hotel, with the exception of maybe dealing with a few intoxicated bar patrons and an occasional crush of late night check-ins from weather delayed airline passengers, things usually slow down and become very quiet during the "wee hours" of the morning. During this quiet time there are very few interruptions and the night auditors typically can finish all of their tasks by 5:00 or 6:00 a. m. before guests start coming down to or calling the front desk. However, when the "books" don't balance, night auditors must continue to work until the problem is resolved.

After the grand opening, business ramped up quickly and we soon experienced many full or almost full houses and the popularity of our location created a booming restaurant and bar business. This increase in business volume was accompanied by an increase in transaction mistakes. Most of these mistakes could be attributed to either new employees' inexperience or simple carelessness by both servers and cashiers in the food and beverage outlets. Whatever the reasons, these mistakes were causing the night auditors to work extra hours to sort out the errors. This extra time started to become a significant problem as it resulted in a noticeable increase in overtime pay.

To remedy the problems, the Assistant Controller and I spent more time training and encouraging both the front office staff and the food and beverage servers and cashiers to pay attention to accuracy. This was something we should have done earlier, but hindsight is always twenty-twenty. As part of the training, one of my instructions was to have the night auditors call me, at any time, if they had a question or made a mistake when trying to post or reconcile any transaction.

This "hands-on" approach helped some, but we were still experiencing way too much overtime to solve the recurring transaction problems. With a bit more analysis, we tracked down part of the problem to how the front office cashiers were recording transactions that were being posted from catering functions.

Spending more time training the cashiers eliminated more mistakes and started bringing down even more of the overtime hours. However, too many mistakes still existed and we just couldn't seem to solve the overtime problem. So, just like with the night auditors, I asked the front office cashiers to call me, at any time, if they had any questions about how to record a transaction.

Being busy with other activities, I don't remember the number of calls I would get to come out to the front desk to discuss particular posting questions, but the volume seemed to be growing. Sometimes my availability to respond to these requests was limited, as I was either out of the office and away from the office phone or wouldn't answer a "call" when talking with a guest or employee. In those situations where the front office cashiers or the night auditors couldn't reach me, they would hold up their work until I returned.

To solve this problem, I gave everyone involved my personal phone number; although this could pose an inconvenience, it would be a worthwhile inconvenience if it would reduce the level of overtime pay. At first, this idea worked very well. I would only get a call when there was a significant problem or question. However, as time went on, I started getting more and more phone calls. It seemed like no one wanted to risk making a mistake, so they began calling me on my personal phone (they said they got a faster response) anytime they were in doubt rather than trying to sort out the problem on their own.

The issue may have been one of not wanting to make a mistake, or it may simply have been easier to call me than make any decisions. Psychologists call this behavior "learned helplessness," and it happens to employees all the time when supervisors start micro-managing. Why should they bother with trying to sort out a problem or make a decision when their supervisor is all too willing to make a decision or do the work for them?

The problem with too many calls came to a head at about 3:00 a.m. on a Thursday morning when a night auditor called to ask if it was okay to change the tape in the adding machine that was almost out of paper. Getting a call on something as trivial as this was my own fault. I had told the night auditors to call me anytime, and I had emphasized ANYTIME, they had a question as I was getting frustrated with the continuing problem of over-time hours. So I couldn't blame them when they called as instructed!

This question was more than just a physical wake-up call in the middle of the night; it was a mental wake-up call as well. Since I was up, I made a pot of coffee and sat down at the kitchen table to think about the evolution of events over the past several weeks. Something was wrong with this situation and, by now, I knew I needed to learn from my mistakes and take corrective actions.

By my actions, I had created a "monster" through my micro-managing. Both the front desk staff and night audit staff had fallen into a pattern of "learned helplessness." In my zeal to solve the problem of preventing recurring mistakes and eliminate the need for overtime hours, I had taken away their desire to make decisions that could result in mistakes and learn from those mistakes.

After a second cup of coffee and a quick shower, it was off to work. Arriving at 6:00 a.m. I greeted the two night auditors with a big smile and said, "Truce, you made your point." After we all had a good laugh about the needless call, it was back to work. What can we learn from this incident?

- Don't create situations of learned helplessness in your employees by insulting their intelligence or always stepping in to do their jobs when problems arise. Involve them in the problem-solving process and help

them solve their own problems, but don't solve all of their problems for them.
- Employees want to know they are important to the organization and have added value in performing their jobs. Micro-managing takes away that feeling of value. Let your employees know that you value them and depend on their ideas by recognizing their creativity and productivity.
- Being a good supervisor requires training employees, equipping them for success and then "letting go" by empowering them to successfully complete their jobs. Recognize that they will make mistakes and learn from those mistakes just as you have while growing in their own self-confidence and sense of responsibility.
- When you make a supervisory mistake, admit it not only to yourself but also to your employees. It's okay to laugh at yourself; it shows you are human. Enjoy your successes, but learn from and grow by acknowledging your mistakes and failures.

In the end, things settled down to a normal routine. After more training and with the experience gained through time on the job, the problem of too much overtime soon cured itself. Everyone became confident in their abilities, learned the importance of working together as a team and performed admirably. The problem in the next chapter was definitely not a routine problem like those found in night auditing, but it was a problem that arose because of a procedural policy.

17

I've Got Pretty Legs

After we got through the excitement of the Grand Opening, and the crush of the first few months of operations, everyone was settling down and some predictability was entering into daily activities. It was fun being busy and when time allowed, we even started doing some cross-training. We were now fully staffed, but we were still being swamped with what seemed like to be a constant never-ending stream of applicants.

As these applicants told us, "the word on the street was that our hotel was a good place to work and paid better than anyone else." The fact was that we were paying a little bit more than our competitors and the added plus of being the newest hotel in town made us a very attractive employer.

In addition, unemployment in the area was high, so walk-in applicants began arriving late in the morning, peaked during mid-day and even continued to trickle in into the evening. In fact, we had so many applicants that the constant flow of foot traffic interfered with normal office operations. So, we decided to limit the hours for accepting applications from

An Accidental Hotelier

10:00 a. m. to 3:00 p. m., Monday through Friday. However, this change in procedures resulted in some unanticipated consequences.

When some job seekers saw the line at or outside of our office door, they simply didn't want to take the time to wait and asked for jobs from anyone they thought looked like a supervisor and might be willing to talk to them about possible employment. For legal reasons, we needed all applicants to apply at one central location so they would all be treated exactly the same.

It wasn't very difficult to get this policy and procedure in place. Supervisors were getting tired of dealing with people who were looking for jobs at all times of the day and night, so they quickly adopted the mantra, "I don't make hiring decisions. You will have to apply at the Human Resource office between 10:00 a.m. and 3:00 p.m. Monday through Friday." Even with our limited hours for taking applications, on a typical day, there would be anywhere from forty to fifty walk-in job seekers who would sign in on the Applicant Log-In Sheet during the first few months after opening.

With this new policy firmly in place, I was surprised when I got a call from the dining room head cashier, Tanya; outside of our posted hours, that there was an applicant I needed to meet. Not wanting to break our established policy for consistency and for legal reasons, I told Tanya that I would come down to the cashiers' station and reiterate our policy on when and where applications could be accepted. Her comment as we hung up, "Good luck with this one," should have served as a fair warning for what I was about to walk in to.

Approaching the cashiers' station, I could see Tanya talking to a fairly attractive woman who was probably in her early to mid-thirties. Tanya introduced me to Sheila and interjected that Sheila insisted that she wouldn't leave until she had talked to someone about a job. I simply did as planned, and explained the hotel's policy on when and where applications were taken and informed her that she would be welcome to return tomorrow during those hours to put in her application.

Sheila was undaunted and quickly explained that she was an experienced cocktail waitress who had just moved to town after working in a very successful nightclub in Atlanta. Since she was new to town and desperately needed a job, she was ready to start working this evening.

Not only was it not the time nor place to take an application, we didn't even have any openings in the lounge or the restaurant for servers. Once again, I told Sheila that she should come back tomorrow and put in an application.

At that point, Sheila said; "You should really hire me, I've got pretty legs." In an instant, she reached down and grabbed the hem of her skirt and pulled it up under her chin.

To my amazement and embarrassment, Sheila was wearing absolutely nothing under her skirt. To say that I was shocked would be an understatement. I stared at her in disbelief, blushed, and was momentarily at a loss for words!

When I finally regained my composure, I asked Sheila to put down her skirt. She said, "Not until you tell me I have pretty legs." I immediately said; "Yes, you have very pretty legs."

With that comment, she dropped her skirt and said, "Will you hire me now?"

Still dumb-founded, all I could say was; "Like I said, please come back tomorrow." At that point, Sheila walked out the door, and, to my relief, she was never seen in the hotel again. Tanya said later as I was jotting down some notes about the details of this incident that, my face turned as "red as a beet." Whoever said; "You can always expect the unexpected," sure knew what they were talking about when it comes to the hotel business.

There was no way to be prepared for this surprise, but there is still much that can be learned from this experience.

- It was never known if Sheila was mentally challenged, under the influence of drugs or alcohol, or if her prank was the act of a person so desperately in need of a job that she had lost her ability to reason rationally. Or, perhaps it was a plot designed to ensnare the hotel in a legal action that was unwittingly defeated by following company policy. Nevertheless, as with the earlier Tarzan incident, whenever you are faced with something that could lead to legal action, follow policy, have witnesses, and be sure to document immediately so that you don't have to depend on your memory to recall facts at a later date!
- Any time policies can be adopted and procedures can be standardized, do so. Establishing and following standard policies and procedures can make jobs easier and insure consistency in everyone's actions.

- Have standardized policies and procedures in place and follow them so that there is never the occurrence or appearance of "playing favorites." Once you have established policies and procedures, stick to them. Making exceptions will lead to trouble. If you make an exception for one person, it may no longer be considered a standard operating procedure.

Sometimes you have to deal with the unexpected and sometimes things come your way that appear to require quick decisions. As you will see in the next incident, it does not always pay to make quick decisions.

18

What a Deal!

The hotel business isn't all that complicated as long as you pay attention to the details every day. This may sound simple, but there are many, many details! And, it has often been said, "If you pay attention to details, the details will take care of themselves." When it comes to the accounting office in a hotel, there are numerous details to be dealt with on a daily basis and then some details that only had to be dealt with on a monthly or quarterly basis. Unlike the night audit, one of the recurring details that always demands attention on a monthly basis is a process called reviewing and aging the accounts receivable. After the paperwork part of this process is completed, attempts are made to collect past due accounts.

The debt collection process begins with reviewing the status of past-due accounts receivable. Once the review process is completed, the next step is sending notices to past due accounts and then as a final step, making collection calls on accounts that are 90 days or more delinquent in payments. Sending out collection letters is an easy-to-complete, straightforward process, but making actual collection calls is usually viewed with trepidation. Even though no one in the office looked forward to making collection calls, it was a process that still had to be done each month. Making a call may sound simple, but if you have never made a collection call, try it some time.

Most people who owe you money don't want to talk to you. When you make collection calls, you will have the opportunity to experience almost every human emotion: disbelief, anger, denial, rage, hate, humility, embarrassment. . . . Sometimes these calls go smoothly and are uneventful, but after making a few tough calls, you just don't really feel like picking up the phone again.

Even though these calls may be difficult at times, making them usually results in success. With a gentle reminder and a little persistence, customers can usually be persuaded to pay their obligations. But, even knowing that you will score some "wins," it is still a difficult task to make one call after another listening to excuses and encouraging people to pay their debts. To give each other encouragement and support in completing this not so fun task, we would always set aside a few hours a month to make our calls at the same time.

During one of these calling marathons to collect past due accounts, Todd, our Purchasing Manager, poked his head in my office and asked if he could interrupt me. I was more than ready to take a break, so I welcomed the interruption. He was obviously excited and immediately burst out with; "I've got a deal that is just too good to pass up!"

"Well, come on, out with it, tell me what it is." He quickly explained that there was a half of a semi-truck load of toilet paper that had become available for immediate delivery and that he could buy it for almost half price if we could take delivery tomorrow. It seems like the original buyer was in financial trouble and could not pay for the order. Although Todd was excited, very excited, I told him to take a breath and slow down. After answering a few basic questions, he assured me that the toilet paper in question was from a reputable wholesaler, met all of our specifications and would provide us with significant long-term savings on a basic necessity we used in large quantities.

The bottom line for this "deal" was that we had to act now and we had to pay for the entire load at the time of delivery. Paying immediately would be a change from our normal practice of only processing invoices for payment either ten or thirty days from receipt based on the discount terms of the invoice. But, we had the authority to make exceptions to that practice on the local level, and this seemed like it might be a good time to make one of those exceptions.

My mind probably hadn't completely shifted gears from making collection calls, but the thought of big savings on a mundane consumable like toilet paper that we used hundreds of rolls each week was very appealing. The price was definitely right, so after a quick review of how much we could save and talking the deal over with the GM, I gave Todd the go-ahead to complete the purchase. I probably should have spent more time discussing this one with the GM, but Todd's enthusiasm was contagious and I reassured the GM that we were making the right decision.

* * *

The events that unfolded in the next few days, made that "knee-jerk" decision to save a few dollars one of the dumber decisions and bigger comedies of events that happened during the early stages of my property level experiences. Do you have any idea how big a half of a semi-truck load of toilet paper is? To put it in perspective, there was enough toilet paper in that load to supply a busy hotel of our size for about three months. That's a whole lot of rolls of toilet paper, especially if storage space is limited, as it is in most hotels.

When the truck backed up to the loading dock and the unloading began, Todd presented me with a new problem. The toilet paper was as promised, but there was just too much of it. I had to "fess up" to the GM about the dilemma our "super special" deal had created. We quickly realized that after filling the housekeeping closets on each floor, there was still so much toilet paper that we were going to run out of storage space. Where were we going to put all of it? Luckily there was a meeting room that would be empty for a few days, but this was not a long-term solution.

The meeting room was scheduled for use the next week and the hotel would be filled to capacity for the next several weeks as we were hosting back-to-back conventions; so there was literally, "no room in the inn" for this windfall load of toilet paper. Since there were no large storage areas in the hotel, there was no place to put our purchase. Remember, you can't generate revenue with storage space, so these non-revenue areas are always minimized in hotel designs. At the GM's recommendation, I rented short-term storage off-property to hold our bounteous supply of toilet paper.

By the time we paid for the storage unit rental, hauled the toilet paper to the storage unit, and then retrieved it in smaller batches with more labor and transportation expenses over the next two months, our "great buy" turned into a "costly misfortune." In the end, we would have been better off sticking to our "on-demand drop shipment agreement" for our toilet paper needs.

In this situation and most others, when something seems too good to be true, it usually is. That was definitely the case with the great toilet paper deal! My dad always said; "When you're faced with a big decision; sleep on it before taking any action." Once again, he was right. In hindsight, this deal was just too good to be true.

My GM never made a comment about the toilet paper fiasco until the storage space had been emptied. He just let me "stew" on my misjudgment and the fact that I had assured him it was a good deal. I returned the same courtesy to Todd. This experience taught all of us some valuable lessons.

- When you are involved in detail oriented tasks that require focused attention, avoid distractions. It is too easy to make mistakes when you are distracted.
- Before you make a decision, make sure you have all of the facts! Consider both the intended and unintended consequences of your decisions. Whenever possible,

allow yourself time to sift through the facts and consider the potential consequences before acting. When something seems too good to be true, it probably is.

- Develop a network of mentors and trusted colleagues that you can use as "sounding boards" and confidants for advice. When faced with big decisions, discuss them in detail with these confidants or someone higher up in the organization, whenever possible, before acting.
- Act quickly, but not too quickly when problems are discovered so that they can be corrected before they become bigger. Seek the advice of others who can help you with their ideas for making things right.
- When faced with a big decision it is always a good idea to "sleep on it" or in other words to "take time to think about" all the alternatives and consequences before acting.

The issue faced in the next incident is a good example of when it would have been a good time to have sought advice and counsel, and waited before acting.

19

False Imprisonment?

The hotel had been open several months, every part of our operations was running smoothly now and our staff was gaining confidence in their jobs. More importantly, our guests were happy and business was booming! It was not uncommon to have lines of guests waiting at times to get into the restaurant and especially the lounge. Daily cash deposits of $5,000 or more for any of the shifts as well as tens of thousands of dollars in credit and debit card transactions was not uncommon. Handling large sums of cash was a financial blessing, but they were also a concern from both a security and internal control perspective.

How was all of this cash handled? Cashiers from the front desk and each of the food and beverage outlets made their deposits into a secure drop slot in a very large secure safe, located away from guest view, in a back section of the front office. On busy weekends, with a lot of food and beverage activity it was not uncommon for over $25,000 in cash deposits to be made over the course of a day and for over $50,000 to be on the property at the end of a weekend.

The safe was opened between 8:00 a.m. and 8:30 a.m. Monday through Friday and the cash would be taken to a back office where the door was locked and cash receipts were verified, and then prepared for bank deposit by the Assistant Controller, or at times, one of the accounting office clerks or myself. The completed deposit would then be placed back in the safe awaiting pickup by a courier from an armored car service. The time of pick-up would vary each day so that for security purposes consistent patterns could be avoided. The courier would also bring in a standing order for small bills and rolls of coins to meet our needs for making change during the day.

When the courier arrived, the safe would be opened and the deposit would be turned over to that person by either myself or the Assistant Controller. In addition to the two of us, the only other individuals who knew the combination and had access to the safe where the GM and the Food and Beverage Director. There was a double-signature log-in that had to be verified by a front-office cashier or night auditor before the safe could be opened, and it was typically opened only by me or the Assistant Controller whenever possible. In fact, since the hotel opened, the GM had never opened the safe and the Food and Beverage Director had only been asked to open it on two occasions.

Cashiers for the front office, restaurant, bar and banquets would pick up their daily banks (cash and coins needed to make change) from lock boxes that were located above the safe at the beginning of their respective shifts. The two busiest shifts for handling cash transactions were the morning, 7:00

a.m. to 3:00 p.m. shift, and the graveyard, 11:00 p.m. to 7:00 a. m. shift. Cash receipts for the 3:00 p.m. to 11:00 p.m., swing shift, were the lightest of all three of the shifts. The graveyard shift had the largest deposits, especially on busy weekend nights, when the bar and restaurant were bursting at the seams.

There was only one more link in these cash transactions. The night auditors on the graveyard shift would reconcile cash, debit and credit card receipts against the actual sales that had been posted each day and either balance these sums or create a discrepancy report that was passed on to the accounting office each morning.

* * *

After we got through the hiccups experienced during our opening and settling in period, these reports had become fairly routine. However, all of a sudden, over one three-week period, we were consistently running $100 short in our cash deposits each of those weeks. The first week this happened, it raised my curiosity, but I didn't become overly concerned, because as we all know, mistakes happen. The second week it happened, I asked the Assistant Controller to see if she could find any explanation for this discrepancy. She could not find anything unusual, but when it happened for the third week, there was no question that something was amiss, and we were both concerned.

With a lot of digging, the Assistant Controller was finally able to isolate the problem to the 7:00 a.m. to 3:00 p.m. front office shift. After we discussed her findings, I asked her to talk to all of the front desk staff that had been scheduled to work that shift. Our normal staffing pattern consisted of two cashiers and two desk clerks on the morning shift. As all of the cashiers and desk clerks had been cross-trained, on occasion when things were especially hectic, one of the front desk clerks could step in to help out the cashiers if things got especially busy. This meant that the possibility of up to four people might have access to the two cash drawers at the desk during the shift. After talking to everyone who might have had access to cash about the problem, there was no closure to the problem, but there were also no shortages for the next three weeks.

Then, just like clockwork, the fourth week after the shortages had stopped, we were once again short exactly $100. When this happened again, I asked the Assistant Controller to do a surprise audit of the cash balances the very next day an hour before the morning shift ended. This turned out to be a good decision, because as one of my good friends often says, "Even a blind squirrel finds an acorn on occasion." Well, this was my lucky day; when she tallied up transactions against the cash on hand, we were exactly $100 short.

The time to act was now! I asked the reservationist and a person from the sales office to cover the front office functions until the next shift arrived and told everyone on the current shift to meet me in room 317. It was a good thing we prided ourselves on cross-training our employees, so covering the front office functions was not a problem. There was no special meaning to this particular room, it was just a "check-out" room that was waiting to be cleaned and selected by the Assistant Controller.

I wasn't sure what I was going to do when I got everybody together, but I just knew deep down in my bones that one of the employees gathered in the room had taken the money. So here we were, the six of us, sitting together in an un-made hotel room and I was livid, as I said, "One of you is stealing money from the hotel!" I know in hind sight that it wasn't my money and this was a foolish move on my part, but I felt violated. My next three statements were probably just as bad. I said, "We are not leaving this room until I find out who has been stealing the money. We have been missing $100 on multiple occasions and this is no coincidence." Then, I said it again, "We are not leaving this room until I find out who is stealing." And, I meant it!

With that said, we all sat in silence, occasionally looking at each other for well over two hours. No one said anything as my four "suspects," were mostly looking down at their shoes. Finally, one of the cashiers said, "You can't keep us here." Then they all chimed in, agreeing, one even saying, "This is false imprisonment." My response, "If you leave, you are fired!" They must have believed me, because no one left and we once again returned to silence and a very thorough examination of the carpet fibers.

Then, out of the blue one of the cashiers said "I've been stealing the money." With that, she reached over and opened her purse and pulled out a $100 bill and handed it to me. I apologized to the other employees in the room, thanked them for their time, and told them to go sign out for the day and that I was looking forward to seeing them tomorrow.

I'm really lucky that in my haste and anger, that I: a) asked the Assistant Controller to join me as three of the front office employees involved in this incident were female, b) no one actually brought any civil action against me, and c) we had all worked together as a team helping each other out with trivial and significant tasks for months, and d) no one was even angry at me. In fact, they were all relieved and thanked me later for exposing someone who was, as one of them put it, "a rotten apple."

The next day was business as usual. Both the Assistant Controller and I spent a great deal of time helping out with the cashiering functions until we could get the schedule adjusted and another cashier hired and trained. I was definitely glad that this experience was behind me, and that there were no adverse consequences. In hindsight, there was a lot to be learned from this incident.

- Don't be impulsive or impetuous in your actions and be aware that stress and fatigue can impair your judgment. Although you may have taken law and human resource management related courses and seminars dealing with commonly faced workplace problems, your instructors may not have prepared you for the unusual types situations created by workplace realities.
- Some of the skills needed to be an effective manager can be learned from analyzing and discussing case studies describing real world situations, but many of

these skills can only be gained through practical on-the-job experiences.
- Do not act in haste, as hasty decisions could lead to unexpected and sometimes expensive consequences. Take a deep breath, maybe even count to ten, and then do it again, before you even think about acting.
- Always remember to document your actions. In case you might be wondering, we took appropriate action and terminated the culprit. She later filed for unemployment and lost, based on her documented admission to theft in front of a group of willing witnesses.

If you think "holding employees" in an empty guest room may have been a foolish decision, wait until you read what happened in the next chapter when we decided to save on payroll expenses during a normally "slow period" for business.

20

Five Minutes of Sheer Terror

There are two givens that you learn early on in the hotel business. First, labor costs are a major expense category and if you want to run a profitable operation, they must be controlled. Do you remember the previous "When in Doubt, Call!" incident and the problem encountered with too much overtime for the night auditors? As that incident demonstrated, payroll costs are a constant concern. Second, there are certain periods of time, even in busy hotels, when business is very slow and occupancy rates drop to almost nothing. Put these two givens together and you face some unique challenges to remaining profitable. The management dilemma becomes one of controlling costs by temporarily reducing staffing to a minimum during times of low occupancy while still maintaining high levels of quality customer service.

In downtown hotels, focused mainly on convention, meeting and business travelers and not leisure travelers, the times of lowest occupancy are typically Thanksgiving and Christmas, when business related travelers are "off the road." This particular Thanksgiving there were reservations for only four of our rooms. If we were lucky, maybe there would be another half dozen "walk-ins," but there wasn't much hope for many more guests. Ten rooms out of several hundred rooms meant we didn't need much staff to meet customer needs.

After an executive committee meeting to discuss the situation, we decided on the rooms side of the business to cut our front office and housekeeping staffing levels to a minimum. However, the food and beverage side of the operations would require a different staffing pattern. There would be a busy brunch and lunch business during mid-day Thanksgiving and then basically die down to nothing until Sunday evening when the hotel would start filling up again, but still not to a high level of occupancy. According to our plans, we would run with a limited kitchen staff, a modified service staff for Thanksgiving brunch and lunch and then cut down to the bare minimum for the remainder of the weekend.

For the rooms side of the operation, one housekeeper would be enough to keep the public areas clean and to take care of guest rooms. The dirty rooms of guests who did check out could wait to be cleaned until business picked up the following week. We would not schedule any hourly employees to work the front desk during the 7:00 a.m. to 11:00 p.m. shifts. Instead, during those two shifts, one member of the management team would provide coverage for each shift. For safety purposes, we would maintain our typical two-person staffing coverage during the graveyard shift. There had been two robberies across the street at a small motel during the wee morning hours when they had only one person on the front desk, and we did not want to put our late-night employees at risk.

I volunteered to cover two of the early shifts and three other unmarried managers who didn't have any family in town or personal commitments volunteered to cover the other shifts. With this group of "volunteers," the hotel would have basic staffing. One manager would cover the front office shifts upstairs and one manager would cover the restaurant and lounge downstairs. For our restaurant and lounge coverage, the restaurant manager would take care of breakfast and lunch and the Executive Sous Chef would cover the evening shift.

Thanksgiving in the restaurant was even busier than we had anticipated and then the next day was quiet, almost to the point of being boring. I had scheduled myself to work the Saturday morning shift since it seemed like nothing would be happening and the quiet time would be perfect for catching up on some paperwork.

* * *

Saturday arrived and everything was going as planned. The restaurant manager stopped by the front desk about 8:00 a.m. to let me know that only one guest had showed up so far. Since everyone was accustomed to high levels of activity, days with little or no business always seemed to drag on forever. He said he would stop back by sometime around 10:00 a.m. to give me a break and then he would stop by again after the lunch period and bring me up something to eat and give me another break. We also agreed that if either of us needed any help, we'd phone.

The minutes and hours ticked by slowly, as if the clock had stopped. The paperwork didn't take long to clean up and I hadn't brought along anything to read. The only thing that broke up the monotony of the soft background music playing through the lobby speakers was one phone call, a wrong number at that.

The only person to walk into the lobby that morning, came in a few minutes before 10:00 a.m. I looked up as the front door opened, about 40 feet across the lobby and was immediately suspicious of my "new guest." It was late November; but remember, we were in the South, and it was unseasonably warm. There was no car or cab at the front entrance, the man had no luggage, was poorly dressed, wearing a baseball cap and sunglasses, and a coat like you would wear on a frigid weather day.

He walked slowly toward the front desk, looking all around as he approached me. I said, "Good morning, may I help you?" and he mumbled something, I couldn't understand in reply. Then, he asked, "Do you have change for a dollar? I need to buy a paper." This was a strange question, because our gift shop was closed and we didn't have any newspaper machines anywhere in the hotel. However, I said, "yes" as he laid a dollar bill on the counter.

I was nervous, very nervous, but tried not to show it. I opened a full-sized cash drawer containing $25 of small bills and assorted change. To my delight, at that very moment, the

An Accidental Hotelier

restaurant manager came bounding up the stairs and briskly strode across the lobby! Help had arrived!

As he approached the desk, he said, "Are you ready for a break?" I immediately said yes, but to my chagrin, he said, "Okay, just as soon as I get some supplies in the back, I'll spell you." Before I could say anything he disappeared in a flash walking around the corner in full stride into the back offices.

All this time our "guest," dressed for 20 degree weather on a 70 degree day kept standing in front of the counter putting the change in his pocket. Then, he pulled a gun from under his coat and said, "Give me all your money." I looked at the barrel of the gun and gingerly pulled all the ones and the two five dollar bills out of the change drawer. There probably wasn't even $20 all together. He said, "Is that all you got?" Bravely or foolishly, I'll never know which, I said, "Yes."

He scooped up the money, stuffed it in his pocket and ran out the front door. As he cleared the second set of doors, the restaurant manager appeared. He said, "I got my stuff, take a break."

My legs couldn't move. They felt like they were made of rubber. All I could say was, "We've been robbed, call the police." He did, and they came. Other than asking me typical questions about the robber's description and how much had been stolen, the only other thing I can remember being asked by the police at that time was, "What kind of gun did the robber have?"

If you have never had a gun pulled on you and pointed in your direction, this may sound like a simple question. If, on the other hand, you have been on the wrong end of a gun, you will understand how silly this question might be. I thought about this question for a moment and said, "It was big and shiny and had a big hole in the end of it." Like I said, don't laugh unless you have been in this type of situation.

As an aside, most businesses as a matter of policy will state that, "an undetermined amount of money was taken," when there is a robbery. Even though they should know exactly how much money was taken, there is no need to advertise how much money is on the premises as stating a specific amount might entice future robberies. Do you remember, the motel across the street had been robbed twice? We always suspected the second robbery happened because the employee who was robbed the first time reported to the newspaper that over $1,500 had been taken!

The rest of the day was a blur. The restaurant manager stepped in to cover my duties and I collapsed into a nearby chair at the reservations desk. The GM arrived just a few minutes after the police arrived and after they had finished questioning me, we had a cup of coffee and we chatted as he debriefed me while taking his own notes documenting the events. One thing we all agreed on after this incident, was that this would be the last time we violated the two-deep policy which was part of our risk management program. Still happy to be alive today, what can we learn from this incident?

- Don't try to be a hero in a robbery situation. Give up the money freely. Life is precious and money can be replaced.

- When policies and procedures call for minimum staffing, these have been developed for a reason. Saving a few payroll dollars isn't worth risking human life!
- To paraphrase Ben Franklin, "You can be penny wise, but pound foolish." Before you change or violate a policy, review and consider why it was initiated in the first place.
- Risk management is serious business. Review and follow all risk management policies and procedures. They could save your life as well as the lives of others.
- Periodically review security procedures with safety in mind. Make sure surveillance systems are current and operating and all procedures and systems have been reviewed by insurance carriers and local law enforcement agencies.

Now that the hotel was operating smoothly, most days seemed to fall into a rhythm with the constant coming and going of guests and an endless parade of people flowing through the meeting spaces and food and beverage areas. However, there was one particular design flaw in the hotel that was starting to become problematic, as you will see in the next chapter.

21

Design Oversights?

Most of you have already read or heard about the legend of Achilles in Greek mythology. In order to make Achilles invincible in battle, his mother dipped him in the River Styx. Since he was being held by his heels in this process, the only part of his body that remained vulnerable in battle were his heels. Legend has it that Achilles was the mightiest of all warriors, but he met his doom when he was eventually shot in the heel during battle with an arrow and ended up dying from his wound.

The story of Achilles and the one small vulnerability of this mythological warrior is interesting, but you might be asking yourself, why this lesson in Greek mythology is important to someone in the hotel business? The answer is simple, everyone and every organization, no matter how great or how well run, has at least one, if not more, failings or weak spots.

With that thought in mind, as you read the rest of this incident, let's see if you can identify anything that might be considered to be the "Achilles heel" of this otherwise beautiful and successful operation. As previously mentioned, we are talking about a very busy downtown convention hotel with an expansive array of meeting rooms and ballrooms.

The number of rooms in this hotel might belie the overall size of this particular property. The meeting and convention space was expansive. The main ballroom could accommodate 1,500 seated at round tables for a served banquet and the secondary ballroom could seat 500 guests. In addition to these two large rooms, there were also four other medium-sized meeting rooms and a very well-appointed board room. We could have definitely used more guest rooms on many occasions to complement the size of the function area, but this was not, "the critical design oversight."

It seemed like the architects had thought of everything when designing this masterpiece. In addition to the expansive meeting rooms and public spaces, there was an attached parking garage that could accommodate almost 700 cars, a high-end restaurant, a high energy live entertainment lounge, a large and nicely supplied gift shop, an exercise room, and an outdoor pool. Being located in the South, an indoor pool was not a necessity. The guest rooms were spacious and had been designed with every comfort in mind. In addition there were also two large sumptuous suites suitable for the most discriminating guests and two well-appointed junior suites.

From all appearances, the interior of hotel had been designed to meet the needs of the most discriminating guests and groups. In fact, the architectural firm that designed the hotel won numerous awards for both exterior and interior design features. It is important to note that experienced hoteliers had not been involved in the initial design of the hotel and our company (we operated the property under a management contract) did not become involved in this project until the foundation had been poured and construction was well under way.

As with any property, we encountered some issues related to design problems as operations began, such as:
- ✓ not enough public elevators to handle peak volume when all of the meeting rooms were in use;
- ✓ only one service elevator;
- ✓ limited storage space;
- ✓ no designated employee break areas;
- ✓ a very long distance to travel between the kitchen and the meeting rooms for banquet service; and
- ✓ every level of the parking garage opened directly onto the first six floors of guest rooms, which caused times of excessive noise, especially at night when banquet traffic was heading to the parking garage.

These may sound like big deals, but every large hotel property faces these and similar design and operational challenges. In time, just like every other hotel management team, we made adjustments and learned to cope with all of these limitations. But, there was a bigger problem, one that everyone had seemed to overlook in the design of the hotel.

Take a moment to look back through the description of the hotel in the past three paragraphs and see if you can discover the "Achilles heel" of this property. There were in fact, two "Achilles heels," one in the room side of operations and one in the food and beverage side of operations. We did not discover the problem in the room side until several months after opening, but the problem in the food and beverage side of operations was noticeable after the first few weeks of opening.

You would never guess the problem on the room side from the clues that have been given, so I'll just tell you. All of the hot water for the guest rooms was supplied by one large boiler located on the top floor of the hotel. None of us had ever thought about this being a potential problem until we experienced a power failure one night when the hotel was completely full. The night auditors were the first to take the brunt of the complaints from angry guests and they were more than happy to leave when it came time to change shifts.

From the number of complaints, it quickly became evident that nobody likes a cold shower. The power failure had tripped the "fail safe" switches that controlled the pilots on our gas-fired boiler, leaving us without hot water in any of the guest rooms from the very early morning hours until late in the morning when the problem was diagnosed and then finally corrected.

Did that little aside give you enough time to think about our design flaw in the food and beverage area? Have you figured it out; or do you give up?

The answer is that there was no quick service restaurant or place to get a snack. This oversight seemed so simple in hindsight, but nobody ever caught it in the design phase. The high-end restaurant was successful at night, but guests had a tendency to shy away from it and breakfast and the lunch business, although adequate, never took off. Maybe this should not have come as a surprise as the furniture and fixtures made it look expensive and the layout was designed with elegant table-side service in mind, not speed.

Our guests just assumed that it was expensive, so even with marketing efforts to nearby offices, potential customers were reluctant to step in the doors. This was a shame as high-volume breakfast business is typically the most profitable meal in foodservice and high-volume lunch business is almost as profitable.

What can we learn from this review of hotel designs?

- Hotels are typically designed by architects and not hotel operators. When architects design a hotel, they often have goals in mind of saving on construction costs or winning awards for beauty. These goals which focus on frugality or aesthetics rather than functionality may overlook important operational considerations.
- Unlike architects, hotel operators are mostly concerned about function and have a tendency to forget about aesthetics.
- If you could get the two sides, architects and hotel operators to sit down and truly listen to each other everyone would win, especially the guests. In the final analysis a team of veteran hoteliers should have the final say in all hotel design issues.
- Marketing is a powerful business tool, but marketing cannot cure design oversights that create customer dissatisfaction. When there is no cure for a design

problem, the only thing you can do is develop and implement a service recovery strategy.

Now, let's move from the physical aspects of the hotel back to the people side of the business in the next chapter.

22

Tanya Who?

Most of you at one time or another have relied on the informal power of the grapevine for getting information that would never pass through formal communication channels. Sometimes the information you get through this informal communication channel is valuable, intriguing, or maybe even titillating, and then sometimes it is just worthless gossip or useless speculation. Whether it passes along useful information, serves as a means of staying in the know, or just provides juicy personal gossip, one thing is for sure, the grapevine is alive, ever-present, and powerful in every organization.

Let me share one simple example of just how powerful and fast-paced the informal grapevine can be (maybe even faster than a text or tweet), especially in a hotel where everyone works together so closely every day. This incident took place about mid-morning on an especially busy day. A State Trooper came to the front desk asking to see an employee. The front desk clerk he approached told him that as a matter of hotel policy, the trooper would need to see someone in human resources in order to "get permission to speak to the employee." It is important to let you know at this point that the front desk clerk was a very close friend of the employee in question.

When I got to the front desk and listened to his request, I told the trooper, "No problem, I'll just walk downstairs with you to the dining room and point out Tanya." This should have been a simple task as Tanya was the Head Cashier for the restaurant and she was always out front at this time of day doing her daily paperwork at the end of the breakfast shift. Tanya, like most employees, had her routine.

When the trooper and I arrived at the cashier's station, Tanya was nowhere in sight. When I asked the hostess, "where's Tanya," her response was, "Tanya who?" I'll admit that sometimes I can be a little slow on the uptake in a social context, but I didn't immediately catch on to what was going on until much later. So, I said, "Tanya Hill." To which the cashier said, "Oh you mean Tanya, she just stepped in to the kitchen."

The trooper and I headed through the dining room toward the kitchen. Stepping through the kitchen door, we immediately ran into the Executive Chef who was standing in the middle of the kitchen and I asked him if he had seen Tanya. His answer was exactly the same as the first one, "Tanya who?"

Still not catching on to what was transpiring, I said, "Tanya Hill." To that, the Executive Chef said, "Oh, you're looking for Tanya. She just came through here heading down toward the banquet area." By this time, I was starting to catch on. As I found out later, all of the employees, and especially Tanya's best friends, assumed the worst. They were thinking that the trooper was there to serve Tanya a summons or worse yet, to arrest her.

Oh, I forgot to tell you that as the trooper and I were on our "wild goose chase" around the hotel, I asked why he wanted to see Tanya. It seems that Tanya's sister had been in a very bad car accident and all she could tell anyone was her sister's name and where she worked. The trooper was trying to locate Tanya so that they could get information to her, and possibly find out if there were other family members and how they could go about notifying them.

When I finally explained all of this to Clarence, our Banquet Manager, who was another one of Tanya's close friends, he said, "Oh, Tanya's at the front desk. Let me call up there and let them know you are coming." And, sure enough, when we got back to the desk, there was Tanya. I am sure to this day, if I had not explained to Clarence why the trooper was trying to find Tanya, we would have still been going around in circles.

The good news was that after a short hospital stay, Tanya's sister was released. And, for a long time after the incident, we all joked about, "Tanya who?" With a happy ending to this incident, what can we learn?

- Formal communication channels are great for disseminating need-to-know facts and information, but informal channels like the grapevine can be just as powerful and a lot faster than formal channels. However, problems can arise when information is passed through the grapevine.

- The grapevine can be a useful as well as problematic form of communication, but never underestimate the power and speed of the grapevine! Continuing changes in technology has even made the dissemination of informal information even faster.
- Learn who in your organization will likely pass along information, those who serve as the "nodes," or those who fill the role as input points for the grapevine and use them. Tap them both when you want to know the "up-to-date scuttlebutt" and also when you want to feed information into this powerful communication medium.
- When employees are "left in the dark," they will fill in the missing information with fact or fiction just as they did in the case with Tanya. In addition, if they are not dealing with facts, then the information that is passed along will probably be embellished in the process.

If we had all been "tuned into the grapevine," we would have seen the events that unfolded in the next chapter much sooner.

23

The Union Knocks

People and organizations are often faced with "tipping points," those seemingly small events that tend to add up until they cause a shift, radically changing the course of future events. One such radical change in events in the lives of all the managers at this new hotel we all considered to be a part of our lives, was the sudden possibility of becoming unionized. Our employees were showing interest in the possibility of being represented by a union regarding concerns about their wages, hours, and working conditions.

Working with unions and unionized employees was nothing new to me. As you may remember from the events in "The Strike" in an earlier chapter, I had some experience with working in a unionized hotel. The flagship hotel and some of the other hotels in the chain had long histories of working with organized labor. While some of the hotels in the chain were also unionized, others were not.

Unionized employees could be found in some of the northern properties, but the new hotels being bought or constructed in southern right-to-work states were all operating as non-union properties. In my opinion, and it reflected the opinions of most managers I know, taking the third party, union representatives, out of operations creates an environment for greater management and operating flexibility. Or, stated another way, it takes some of the "hassles" out of managing. To be fair, other managers would disagree as they have always worked in this type of environment and seem to enjoy it.

To achieve and maintain the goal of operating non-union properties, great efforts were taken to match or exceed pay scales and benefits of all local hotels. When we opened the hotel, we had an established pay scale that was a few percentage points more than any of our competitors and a benefits package that included health insurance as well as one more paid holiday and more vacation time after five years of service.

These benefits were a bit more generous than those being offered by the competitors we considered to be our peers. The only two things that could be considered missing from the benefits package were a pension plan and dental insurance.

Not having these two benefits didn't seem to be a problem as none of our competitors offered them either. So with very competitive pay and a decent benefits package, we were surprised when we learned that union organizers were present.

One organizer was particularly noticeable as he could be seen handing out literature and "representation cards" for signatures just off the hotel property at the back entrance where most of our employees entered and exited the hotel. This experience became a "tipping point" for every manager in the hotel.

Maybe this organizing attempt should not have come as a surprise as we were operating in a very unionized city where many manufacturing employees were represented by some of the largest and most powerful unions in the country. However, unions were not common in the services industries and none of the lodging properties in the city had any union representation.

What we soon learned about the organizing attempt was that our hotel had been "targeted." There were only two other large hotels in the city, and, for reasons we did not understand, we had been selected as the first hotel that should be organized for union representation. Of the other two hotels, one was locally owned and operated and the other was part of a large national chain. Although there had been some organizing activity at the second property, we were the primary target for organizing.

As we later learned, it had been determined that our city had been identified as a prime target for "green field" hospitality union organizing. The union's strategy was for our hotel to be organized first, and since our corporate parent had a long history of union representation at the flagship hotel, we were a perfect target. In the union organizers' plans, once we were organized, their campaign would move on to the large national chain hotel and then to the locally-owned hotel. Funding was available to organize our hotel, and funding for future campaigns was to come out of dues from our employees when a contract was signed.

This strategy may have seemed simple from the union's perspective, but there was one problem with it. Management at the corporate level had decided that they did not want to operate any more unionized hotels and they were determined to fight this organizing campaign. So began yet another learning saga.

* * *

As the GM gathered all of the management staff together at the beginning of the second week after discovering the organizing efforts, we learned that we had been doing some things right all along, but we still had a lot to learn. We would be fighting an uphill battle in this campaign as wages were higher in some of the northern properties and many of our employees had family members or friends who had union jobs in the manufacturing sector which paid higher wages and offered more benefits. The organizers where promising that they could do the same for our employees.

On the management side, our coach and guide through this process was an experienced labor law attorney who specialized in representing employers during union organizing campaigns. We quickly learned that the union representatives could do or say almost anything, but we were very restricted in our actions. In the process of learning what we could say to employees, we learned a very important acronym. That acronym, **TIPS** (**T**hreaten, **I**nterrogate, **P**romise and **S**py), quickly became part of our everyday thoughts.

Having **TIPS** constantly on our minds helped us to remember those things that we could not do or say when interacting with nonexempt employees (those employees potentially eligible to be part of the bargaining unit). These restrictions included doing or saying anything that could be considered as a **T**hreat against them for participating in organizing activities; an **I**nterrogating question about union activities; a **P**romise in return for voting against the union; or, anything that would be considered **S**pying on union activities.

Doing any of these things could have resulted in the filing of an unfair labor practice on the part of the union and could have led to recognizing the union even without a vote. Oh, one of the very important things we had been doing right all along was holding departmental and all-employee meetings on a regular basis. This meant that we could still hold meetings with employees to discuss our views on unionization, and these would not be considered "captive meetings," another potential unfair labor practice.

There are a lot more details that could be mentioned about the campaign from both sides, but suffice it to say, these were emotionally tense times. Employees were suspicious of every management action and the "fun loving" atmosphere of "we are all in this together" and "let's do whatever it takes to please the customer" we thought we had, disappeared during the weeks leading up to the election. Again, to be fair, both sides in this election had some valid points and the techniques used to sway voters was as intense as can be found in any political campaign.

During the campaign the GM, Food and Beverage Director and I became the voices of the company. The employees liked and trusted both the GM and the Food and Beverage Director and I knew all 350 of our regular employees by name since I had been involved in their hiring and orientation as well as being the person they often came to with questions about pay, benefits, training and promotion opportunities. I had also made it a point to stop by every department on each shift to talk with employees since the day we opened. The employees had my trust and I felt obligated to keep that trust.

When the election was finally held, the management side prevailed, but just by one vote. The good news was that after the election, we had time to work on the areas where our employees had expressed concerns, but the bad news was that the union only had to wait for one year and a day before they could resume organizing efforts again if they so desired. We definitely had work to do if we wanted to remain non-union.

What were the employees' concerns? Pay? No. Benefits? No. The main concerns they voiced were centered around seniority issues: seniority in scheduling and vacation choices. These seemed like easy concerns to address, so we set out to consciously and systematically take seniority into consideration in all of our staffing pattern decisions immediately.

In the final analysis, the primary reason the razor-slim majority of our employees said that they decided to vote in favor of management, was that they trusted us to do the right thing. Keeping that sense of trust was an important burden that had to be honored if we were to remain a non-unionized property. In addition to being humbled by this thought, what else can we learn from this experience?

- Trust is hard to earn, easy to lose, and once lost, even harder to rebuild.
- If you do not operate in a unionized environment, you could at any time. Management mistakes, combined with failing to listen to and respond to legitimate concerns, can lead employees to seek the security, protections, and benefits promised by unions. When management loses its focus on employee needs and concerns, the union is always there ready to help.
- Although your position as a manager gives you legitimate power to both reward and punish employees, it is your demonstrated expertise in dealing with people and your personal ability to motivate and empower people that creates employee respect, commitment and trust.
- It has often been said that, "Unionized hotels deserve to be unionized." This can probably also be said for any organization that fails to truly listen to their employees and address their concerns.
- Establish a regular schedule of employee meetings at the departmental level and the property level and stick to it. During these meetings create an environment of two-way communication, providing updates, training and other useful information as well as actively listening and responding to suggestions for operational improvements.

- If you remember nothing else from this incident, remember **TIPS**. The four reminders that make up this simple acronym can keep you out of a lot of trouble if you are ever faced with a union organizing attempt.

Not every situation you deal with will be as challenging as an organizing campaign, but every day you will be faced with dilemmas and decisions, both large and small as you will see in the next chapter.

24

Ouch!

This short incident may not seem like a big deal, but it is! As it will demonstrate, honesty can be painful, but in the end, if you are honest, you will feel better about yourself.

Ethics is taught in many upper level college courses and for good reason. You will be faced with many ethical dilemmas, both big and small, in business and in life. Many of these dilemmas will be big issues like the ones discussed in those college classroom examples, but many of the ethical dilemmas we face in life are not that big, popping up during the daily course of work.

Realizing that ethical decision-making in an everyday part of life, ask yourself some very simple questions whenever you are faced with a situation or problem that could lead to an ethical dilemma.

- ✓ Will someone be hurt in this situation?
- ✓ Is anyone being coerced, manipulated, or deceived?
- ✓ Is there anything illegal about the situation?

- ✓ Does the situation feel wrong to you?
- ✓ Is someone else telling you that there is an ethical problem?
- ✓ Would you be ashamed to tell your best friend or see a story about your contemplated actions or involvement spread across Facebook or other social media accounts?

Here are the facts of the situation. As you already know, the hotel handled a very large volume of cash transactions on any day and on occasion we would run into a stray counterfeit bill. Even with proper training and procedures, the possibility of getting a counterfeit bill is just one of the costs of doing business, especially when your cashiers are handling large numbers of transactions. I'm sure the Assistant Controller could have made the decision herself in this situation, but since it was a little bit out of the ordinary, she laid it at my feet.

While counting and preparing the deposit slip for the previous day's cash transactions, she noticed five $100 bills that looked a little suspicious. Even though they passed all of the typical tests, they just didn't seem to be 100% right. Since they passed all of the normal tests and nothing indicated that they were counterfeit other than our own "gut level" feel from handling a lot of money, she posed a two-answer question.

Should we both ignore the feeling we had about these being counterfeit bills and put them in with the deposit or should we hold them out of the deposit and take them to the bank for verification? If we were wrong about our suspicions and if we left them in the deposit, maybe no one would notice. If we were right about our suspicions and took them to the bank, by law they would be confiscated and the hotel would lose $500.

The choice was straight-forward, as there were only two options. What would you have done? Before you make your decision, go back to the previous page and look at the list of questions for making ethical decisions.

When you review the questions presented in the list above, you will quickly notice that you can answer yes to almost every one of them. So, without a whole lot of thought, we both agreed to hold the bills in question out of the deposit and I took them to the bank later that morning to verify their authenticity.

We were correct to be suspicious as the bills did prove to be counterfeit and were confiscated. Ouch, we were out $500, but our decision had been ethical!

What can we learn from this seemingly minor issue?

- No matter how big or small the ethical dilemma, acting ethically in every situation is important to your career success.
- Being ethical is a lot like telling the truth, always do the right thing and tell the truth. That way you never have to question what you have done or remember what you have said.
- If you are willing to be unethical in small matters, chances are you will act unethically when the stakes are bigger. Don't risk your career by acting unethically in any situation.

There are many more learning experiences to explore, but in the next chapter we take a break from dealing with day-to-day operational issues and focus instead on the importance of self-evaluation.

25

Focusing on a Career Plan

My GM and everyone I encountered from the corporate office had always encouraged me to think about where I wanted to go with my career. That was how I had found myself working at the property level. It must have shown that I didn't see any clear future for myself in my current position. Most of the suggestions for my future focused on taking the necessary career steps to becoming a hotelier. Fred, the Assistant Controller for the corporation and one of my early mentors, had a different idea. He really encouraged me to consider at some point coming back to the corporate office, but he would always qualify this statement with that one nagging caveat I had heard so many times before. He said if I wanted a future in the corporate office, then I needed to become a Certified Public Accountant (CPA). To do that, I would need to take more accounting courses and then pass the CPA exam.

You might think that I should have been able to make up my mind by now, but I hadn't. Still being a little undecided about my long-term future, I decided to explore all options and was admitted to a local university and registered for a night course in an advanced accounting subject. This seemed like a good idea at the time; however, after working some long hours, many times six days a week, I didn't have the time, energy, or enthusiasm to devote to studies. After just two weeks, I knew this approach to continuing education was not going to work, so I dropped my course.

Then came a great deal of soul-searching and many conversations with mentors. It seemed like almost everyone involved in my career development thought that with my educational background and operations experience, it might be a good idea to continue pursuing the CPA option. There was, however, no consensus on how I should go about doing this. A part-time approach had proven to be out of the question.

Finally, after many discussions, a possible alternative was decided on. All of us, from my GM to the Vice President of Human Resources at the corporate office agreed that the best approach would be to take an indefinite unpaid leave-of-absence to pursue the needed coursework to obtain my CPA. To provide financial support for this planned course of action, I found a teaching position at a small college where I could simultaneously teach and audit accounting courses to get myself back "up to speed" in required accounting classes.

During this leave, I kept in touch with the corporate office and, in a time of need, I invested a week of my time assisting the management staff at another one the chain's hotels during another union-organizing attempt. The more accounting classes I took, the more I realized that my heart was really in operations and not in accounting. So, after a brief two-year stint at teaching management and simultaneously auditing accounting courses, I wanted to get back into operations. As I had been told on multiple occasions, I had a bright future with the organization, but needed to decide where I wanted to focus. Finally, at this stage of my career, there was no question, I wanted to do whatever it took to become a hotelier.

The VP of Human Resources and I discussed my options. One option was to return to the corporate office and continue working on special projects, but there would be no clear career path without the CPA. A second option would be to fill an open position similar to the previous one I had held in one of the hotels when it became available. A third option would be to return to my old hotel in a different position. There was no question that having developed a reputation of coming to work early, staying late, and volunteering to do more than necessary, was paying off when it came to opportunities within the organization.

As the VP of Human Resources had been exploring possible placements and sharing my resumé; my old GM said he really wanted me back; this time, as an Assistant Manager with the long-term thought of getting me the necessary experience to eventually be promoted to a General Manager position. The hotel had never had an Assistant Manager, as these duties had been shared by members of the management team who assumed many of these types of duties on a rotating basis in the role of "manager on duty." However, after a few years of operations, the GM had decided that the management team was being stretched too thin and more depth and coverage was needed, especially since the original Food and Beverage Director (and de-facto Assistant Manager) had moved away.

This opportunity fit perfectly with what I now envisioned as my long-term goal of becoming a hotelier, and I was ready to be back in hotel operations. There was still a lot to learn, but I knew one thing for sure: getting back in to hotel operations would be challenging, rewarding, exciting, and fun! This experience is probably unique, but it offers an opportunity to think on a personal level about careers and career options. With that in mind, what can we learn from these experiences?

- Consciously plan your career even if you later make changes; don't leave career planning to a last minute decision. Career planning should be a continuous process involving you, your supervisor(s), mentors and members of the human resource staff.
- Maintaining good communications with your mentors and superiors, and not "burning bridges," is an important part of your career development.
- The hotel business is big, but at the same time it is a surprisingly a "very small world." You never know when past relationships may provide unexpected opportunities. It is not just a cliché, but a fact, that career paths often cross and everyone who works in the hotel industry soon learns that it is a "very small world" and everybody seems to know everyone else.
- Too often employees pursue other job opportunities and fail to discuss their future options with their current employer. If you are unhappy or frustrated in your current position, then explore the possibility for a

change with a trusted mentor whose sphere of influence could potentially open a career enhancing position with your current employer.
- Never make a career decision that involves changing employers without giving your current employer an opportunity to share their plans for your future.
- Develop a reputation as a team player who comes in to work early, stays late, and volunteers to do more than necessary without being asked.

Returning to my old hotel, as you will see in the next chapter, was a bittersweet experience.

26

Something Didn't Seem Right

It was like old home week when I returned to the hotel. After being on leave for over two years, it was exciting to return to the hotel I had helped open. Returning to the hotel would give me a chance to work with several people I knew and respected, especially the GM. Many of the people I had worked with including sales office employees, desk clerks, housekeepers, cooks, servers, dishwashers, reservationists, and food and beverage outlet managers were still there. It was good to be working with old friends and acquaintances in familiar surroundings. The only senior personnel who had left were the beloved Food and Beverage Director and Executive Chef. They had both opened the hotel and been with the management team that had gone through the union organizing campaign.

FYI

New hotels are always opening and being developed so the demand for employees seems to be never ending. When it comes to staffing, the hotel business is known for two very different but related phenomenon. First, the business is known for a high level of turnover, especially in hourly and entry-level supervisory positions. So, you will always be looking for new employees. Second, the business is also known for preparing people to move on to new positions. Sometimes this means moving to another hotel and at other times this means an internal promotion. Hotel managers pride themselves on promoting from within whenever possible. When you work closely with people, it is always sad to see them go, but it is also a time of celebration when promotion opportunities arise from within.

However, soon after returning to the hotel, my euphoria was quickly dampened. Nancy, who had taken my previous position as the hotel's controller, asked me if I had time for a cup of coffee and a few questions. When I suggested we go down to the restaurant, she said she had a pot in her office and wanted to talk in private.

When she shut her office door, her first words were, "You and I have known each other for a long time and I need to talk to someone I can trust (these were ominous words). I'm not sure, but I think we may have a problem in our food and beverage department." She went on to explain that for the past several months, food costs had been anywhere from 2 to 3% over budget. I agreed that it sounded a little high if it were on a consistent basis, but not all that bad. She quickly responded, that much deviance could amount to over $50,000 or more in a year in lost profits.

As we continued to talk, I asked if she had talked about her concerns with Conrad, the new Food and Beverage Director. She assured me that she had done this on several occasions. His response was the cost differentials were a result of the catering sales staff cutting too many special deals to attract business when finalizing prices for banquets. My next question was obvious. Does his reasoning make any sense? Her response was firm. "No, it doesn't. I've been working with Ryan, the Accounts Payable clerk, to cost out banquet food sales, and according to last month's costs, we should have been below budget."

Not being sure exactly what to do at this point and seeing that Nancy was not only frustrated, but also a little hot under the collar, I asked her if she had shared her concerns with the GM. She said that she had and that both the GM and Conrad had concluded she was, "Spending too much time counting pennies and not to worry as long as the food and beverage department remained profitable and food costs held steady." With that, I told Nancy I would do a little investigating on my own and based on my finding, talk with the GM about her concerns, if they seemed warranted. At her request, I also assured her that I would keep her name out of the discussions since Conrad had been accusing her of being out to get him.

As the Assistant Manager, I had access to all of the information in the operation, even though my primary responsibilities were for Rooms Department operations. Both Conrad and I had the same reporting relationship to the GM, but in the GM's absence; officially, as was the practice with the previous Food and Beverage Director, Conrad was placed in charge of all operations. Hence, in the normal course of business, I did not spend much time with food and beverage operations.

The opportunity to discuss food and beverage costs came up sooner than expected when the GM asked me if there were any items I wanted to have included on the biweekly executive committee meeting agenda. I mentioned that I would be interested in discussing food and beverage costs since they were the only cost categories consistently over budget. I was surprised when he said that I must have been talking to Nancy. I admitted that she had made some comments to me about her concerns with food costs, but that I had also been doing some investigating on my own and had discovered what I thought might be a potential problem.

I was surprised and at the same time troubled when the GM cut the conversation short by saying that he had complete confidence in Conrad and did not want the subject of food costs brought up again. I definitely felt like I was in a difficult position. This was the GM, who had hired me to open the hotel, brought me back into his management team after my leave of absence and a person for whom I had great respect. He had been my mentor and, over the years, we had developed a strong working relationship and friendship. But at the same time, I also valued Nancy's ability to zero in on potential trouble spots.

I could have walked away from this food and beverage issue, I decided not to do so. This decision was probably an artifact of my internal auditing experiences. I adjusted my schedule to spend more time observing activities in the food and beverage department. With these schedule changes, Conrad must have sensed my increased presence because he openly complained at the next executive committee meeting that I was spending way too much time in the food and beverage areas. Although Conrad protested, the GM encouraged me to learn as much about food and beverage as possible to prepare myself for future promotion opportunities.

Two months passed before I brought up the subject of food costs again. On a quiet Saturday morning (he had a habit of always coming in for a few hours on Saturday or Sunday), I stepped into the GM's office armed with a full set of notes. I told him that I was still concerned about our food and beverage operations and needed to share those concerns.

I began by telling him that I thought Nancy was right; there seemed to be something that wasn't right in those areas. I still wasn't sure what it was, but I thought the problem might be bigger than just a cost issue. With that lead-in, I shared some of the things I'd picked up over the past two months. First, Conrad, Jeff (the new Executive Chef), and Peggy (the new Purchasing Agent) had all worked together at another hotel before coming here. In fact, Jeff and Peggy were hired on Conrad's recommendations.

Second, six months ago, Conrad hired his brother, Larry, as a relief cook to work on weekends and to help out on extremely busy nights with banquet preparations even though Larry had no previous culinary experience. Larry's regular job was working as a maintenance helper for an apartment complex. The fact that they were related and working in the same department was a violation of the hotel's nepotism policy. Conrad, had shrugged off the nepotism concern, telling me the nepotism policy didn't apply to temporary help. Conrad said that, "It's a good arrangement because Larry only works when needed and Jeff can depend on him."

Third, eight months ago, we stopped purchasing from Premier Meats, here in town, and began purchasing all of our meat and some frozen products from Carver Meats located over 200 miles away. Conrad and Peggy both said that with this change in purveyors, we were getting the same quality product and service at a better price. Comparing old invoices from our previous purveyor with our new purveyor, the quality appeared to be the same, but the prices were several pennies higher per pound.

Fourth, Wendell, the storeroom clerk, told me that the night cooks were concerned because, on several occasions, Larry has used the Chef's keys to get supplies from the storeroom without the required requisitions. The night cooks were afraid to say anything to Conrad or Jeff, but the cooks were also afraid of being blamed if anything was discovered to be missing.

Finally, the night before, I was working late to assist with taking the end of the month inventories. When I went to the kitchen, Peggy and Larry were taking inventory. When I asked Peggy where the Chef or the Executive Sous Chef were, she told me that they were both busy so she asked Larry to help her take inventory. This procedure seemed odd, so I stayed late and spent some time with the night audit crew. After the kitchen shut down and the food and beverage outlets were closed, on a hunch, I re-inventoried the meat coolers. The counts and weights I got were less than those reported on Peggy and Larry's inventory sheets.

After going through this list of concerns and inconsistencies with the GM, the response I got surprised me. All he said was, "Conrad told me you have been snooping around." Then he went on to say that it sounded like all of the things I'd found were just judgment calls. Maybe Conrad was right, "He thinks that the two of you have a personality clash resulting from your envy of his position and the strong support he gets from his staff." It was true that Conrad was a very charming, even an engaging, if not charismatic individual, who was instantly likable. Angrily I told the GM that we had known each other for way too long and that he knew better. In fact, I was so sure of myself that I told him to call the VP of Food & Beverage and let him look into the situation if he wasn't sure about my concerns.

* * *

Monday afternoon, after that Saturday meeting, I got a call to come to the GM's office. When I arrived, the GM and Conrad were discussing food costs. Much to my surprise, the GM asked me to summarize the facts I had presented on Saturday morning. Conrad was very dismissive of my concerns, providing reassuring responses; calmly giving plausible reasons for any problems or concern presented.

Finally, at the end of what became a very heated discussion, Conrad told the GM to keep me out of his operations because my continual questioning and snooping were becoming disruptive. The outcome of this meeting was that the GM gave me very definite instructions to limit my future involvement in the food and beverage areas.

Feeling a bit let down and perhaps even betrayed after this meeting, I decided to vent my frustrations with Nancy. I had visited with Nancy many times during my investigation to ask her questions and get accounting information related to my concerns. However, this was the first time I had a detailed discussion with her about what I had discovered. After recounting the events of the past few weeks, Nancy and I agreed that there was a problem, but we were not sure what to do next.

I was still fuming about our heated meeting, and believed the GM was being deceived, but I followed orders and stayed away from food and beverage operations as much as possible. What I didn't know at the time, was that Nancy had called Fred, the Assistant Controller for the Corporation, and shared both of our concerns. Fred had then shared this conversation with the VP of Food and Beverage, and two days later, I got a phone call.

The VP of Food and Beverage was in town and wanted to meet me for lunch at a restaurant a few blocks from the hotel. When I arrived, he was with the VP of Operations and the GM. Something big was brewing, but let's save that for the next chapter, and reflect on what can be learned from this incident.

- When you sense that something is not right, carefully and thoroughly investigate and document your findings. If you are sure of your facts, don't be intimidated into ignoring those feelings and facts and not reporting potential problems.
- Always tell the truth. Don't protect someone who has done wrong and inadvertently become a co-conspirator.
- People can lie, but numbers don't. When confronted with suspicious behavior rely on facts and don't be fooled by personalities.
- When something is wrong and those in charge will not take corrective action, as a last resort, blow the whistle! Even if you lose your job, and you shouldn't, as there are laws designed for your protection, you will have maintained your integrity. Once again, keep

more than one copy of the documented details of your findings in more than one location.

By sticking with my principles and knowing right from wrong, I unknowingly became a change agent. What that change would mean to my career soon became evident in the next chapter.

27

A Radical Change in Job Descriptions

I'm not sure what I expected when I became a whistle-blower, but what was about to happen came as a shock. Meeting with two senior members of the corporate management team and my GM, off-property, was a little unnerving. I had been off-property with members of the senior corporate management team before, but on those occasions, we were always one-on-one and scouting out other hotels or restaurants to evaluate their service offerings. This time, the dynamics were very different.

After some brief pleasantries and updates on my family, (I had married that beautiful young lady who was a witness with me to the Tarzan adventure at the Grand Opening), the VP for Food and Beverage asked me a very pointed question. "Would you be willing to step in as acting Food and Beverage Director for a couple of months?"

I was completely surprised. Other than observing and helping out with menial tasks like plating food for large banquets when things got really busy, I had no real food and beverage experience. The fact that my GM and members of the corporate management team thought I was capable of managing a multi-million dollar food and beverage operation was a bit overwhelming.

When I asked, "What about Conrad?" The response was somber. He, along with Jeff and Peggy would no longer be with the hotel at the end of the day. In fact, as I found out later, at that very moment we were meeting, the VP of Human Resources and Nancy, the hotel controller, were conducting exit interviews with all three of them. This brief, but poignant response, confirmed my suspicions that there were probably more problems than I had imagined.

My job description was about to radically change. Before the meeting was over, I accepted the position of Food and Beverage Director with the understanding that the job would only be temporary. There were also assurances that I would get full assistance and support from the corporate office.

It was already the end of the lunch shift when we returned to the hotel, and the VP of Human Resources and Nancy had already gathered everyone in the current food and beverage shift in the dining room. It felt like a very awkward moment, but I'm not sure there would have been any other way to let the staff know that there were going to be some major staffing changes.

An Accidental Hotelier

The GM made the announcement that I would be the new Food and Beverage Director. Then he went on to explain that there had been some other changes that day. There were several questions that he really couldn't answer since they were personnel-related, but he reassured everyone that this would be a smooth transition and that the VP of Food and Beverage would remain on property for the next few days to help with the transition. Surprisingly, after the initial shock, the questions and generally mumblings died down, and with that brief announcement, I embarked on what I thought would be a new short-term assignment.

My comments to the assembled group were that we were all in this together and that I would need their support and cooperation for us to succeed. With that said, everyone, probably a little shaken and bewildered, returned to their normal duties. The hotel was full and there was a big banquet scheduled for that evening. Everyone was busy and there wasn't much time for idle gossip. We repeated this same type of meeting with similar responses as the evening shift arrived.

The first weeks in the new job were a little bit shaky, but with the support and encouragement of the staff and my wife, who knew a lot about food and beverage operations, my confidence in performing daily tasks grew each day. It helped that I already knew all the employees and, for the most part, they were eager to help me succeed. Another plus to my success, was that not one key staff member left over this incident.

Two months turned into a year and then two years. I kept asking when they were going to hire a professional Food and

Beverage Director. The answer was always, "Don't worry, we are looking for one. Be patient."

I was finally told that they had never really looked very hard for a replacement. They were pleased with what was happening from an operational perspective and, after a few months of positive financial results, they just quit looking. Our costs had returned to normal and, with a few exceptions, our customer comments were always in the good to excellent ranges. Why should they have put any effort into making any changes?

Big, almost seismic changes may not be all that common in the workplace, but they do happen. Even if you are never confronted with a situation of this magnitude, there is still much that can be learned from these experiences.

- Job opportunities sometimes appear unexpectedly and may not be part of your planned career path. If those you respect think a new job opportunity would be good for you, even if you think you may not be qualified, seriously consider accepting it!
- Don't be afraid of an opportunity even if it involves a physical move or taking on new and unfamiliar tasks that may seem intimidating. You can learn new job skills outside your "comfort zone" and area of expertise, so don't be afraid to continue learning and growing professionally.
- Although support is often promised, it sometimes does not materialize. Be prepared to "stand on your own two feet" and rise to the occasion.

- You may think your career path is set, but circumstances outside of your control can result in new directions that no one ever anticipated. The hotel business is full of stories about unexpected career changes, and most of these career changes result in positive outcomes.

As you will read in the next several chapters, moving into food and beverage operations provided some very unique and interesting learning experiences. These things didn't happen all at once, but occurred over the course of time.

28

Dumpster Diving

There are some tasks, especially in food and beverage operations, that are just disgusting! Anyone who has worked in the kitchen knows or maybe has even had the opportunity to do a few of these tasks; cleaning out grease traps and unplugging garbage disposals on dish machines probably top most people's lists. However, the task that I am about to describe may be even worse.

As previously mentioned, the hotel had a very upscale restaurant. One of the many fine touches that set this restaurant apart from others was the linen and tableware. The handle of each knife, fork, and spoon was emblazoned with the corporate logo. To keep inventories at minimum levels, we also used the same tableware in banquets. Therefore, it was not uncommon to have well over 3,000 of each of these pieces of tableware in use and in stock at any given time.

If you are not aware of it, people like to collect spoons with logos on them. We anticipated this type of loss into our usage patterns and would always order 20% more spoons than knives or forks when we replaced our par stocks of these items. This may seem like a big expense, but we considered it to be part of our marketing program, hoping that it would create top-of-mind name recognition and positive word-of-mouth publicity as people talked about their experiences at our hotels.

FYI

You might be surprised at the "souvenirs" guests like to take away as mementos of their stays. Things like soap, shampoo, hair conditioner, body lotion and ball point pens are to be expected. Even the occasional wash cloth or maybe even a pillow, coffee carafe, spoon or flower vase might not be a surprise. But, how about this next one. Walking through the public areas one evening, I ran into a man and woman who were carrying out a cocktail table from the lounge. When I asked them what they were doing, the woman simply said, "this would look great in our family room." At that point, they simply put it down and walked away. I guess, if something is not bolted down to the floor or wall, some people might consider it to be fair game, and available for the taking.

You can't talk about silverware losses and other inventory shrinkage without also considering employee turnover. Now, you might think, what do employee turnover and silverware have in common? To answer that question, you have to realize that no matter how tight your loss prevention controls might be, some employee will steal anything they think has value or that they might use.

One of the things common to all foodservice operations is the fact that food, silverware and many small items (called small wares) just disappear, an occurrence referred to as, "shrinkage." Once those employees who are intent on stealing have taken enough to meet their "needs" and the "needs" of their friends and relatives, or they finally get caught and are terminated, the rate of loss should decrease. Therefore, when employee turnover decreases, so does "shrinkage" of silverware as well as other small wares. So, in addition to reducing training costs and improving customer service, the cost of consumables also decreases with lower levels of turnover and that in turn leads to greater profitability.

Another problem, that is always hard to control with silverware, is that some of it just gets thrown into the garbage through laziness or carelessness by dishwashers and those who are bussing tables. This is especially problematic with large banquets that run late into the night. In their hurry to get everything cleaned and set-up for the next day, employees often take shortcuts that lead to losses by throwing silverware, napkins, and other small wares in the garbage.

During the height of our fall banquet season, it was becoming obvious from the number of purchase orders I was signing that we were losing extraordinarily large amounts of tableware and napkins. On one of those very busy nights when the dining room was full and every banquet room was filled to capacity, I happened to walk past the back loading dock as trash cans from one of the banquets were being emptied. Right on top of the dumped load were two forks, a spoon and three napkins!

I immediately told the banquet staff to stop dumping any garbage and went to find the banquet manager, Clarence, to talk about this problem. There were still three garbage cans to be dumped, and my suspicion was that there would be more silverware, napkins and probably some salt and pepper shakers as well in these cans.

When the two of us arrived at the back loading dock, the two employees who had brought the cans to be dumped were still there. After a brief discussion, Clarence assured me that it was just a mistake and he would instruct his employees to be more careful. I wasn't that reassured and asked Clarence if he thought there would be any other silverware or napkins in the garbage cans waiting to be dumped. His answer was no, so I said, "If we dump these cans and there is anything of value in any of them, we'll both go dumpster diving tonight."

Sure enough, the cans were dumped and there were more knives, forks, spoons, and napkins. I kept my promise. In my suit and tie, I hopped into the dumpster, and started pulling out discarded tableware and napkins plus a couple of salt and pepper shakers. Clarence was reluctant to come in the dumpster with me, but I reminded him of his promise. So in he came, and, the more we dug, the more we found. It was messy experience, but it truly was leadership by example!

You may have noticed that I didn't ask the banquet employees to join us. They just stood and watched. That was the plan! I wanted Clarence to understand how serious this problem was and to spend more time in training and supervision. The plan worked! I told Clarence when we had finished with this adventure that we would do it again if I or anyone else noticed valuables being tossed in the garbage.

If you have never jumped into a dumpster-full of a day's trash from a busy foodservice operation, it is an experience that you might want to avoid. That pair of shoes and my suit were salvaged after a good cleaning and some valuable lessons were learned.

- Be vigilant! "Shrinkage," especially of food, silverware, and other small wares is a fact-of-life in the hotel business. Pay attention to the details and the details will take care of themselves!
- Lead by example. Don't ever ask employees to do something that you wouldn't do yourself. These tasks may range anywhere from cleaning toilets or grease traps to washing dishes or taking out the trash. No job should ever be beneath you no matter how high up in the organization you rise. Remember, in the hotel business, you can't manage by sitting behind a desk.
- Show employees that you are willing to "get your hands dirty" and that you not above doing menial or even disgusting tasks. Employees will respect your

commitment, take more pride in their work and feel more a part of the team.
- Don't get to the point where you need to jump into dumpsters. In meetings with your employees, clearly communicate the importance of controlling costs and establish a reward system for consistently good results. However, unannounced, still monitor the dumping of a few trash cans to confirm that policy is being followed.

You have already observed the need for being flexible, planning, and paying attention to details in the hotel business. The next chapter reinforces those themes, but with a surprising twist.

29

Best Laid Plans

Planning is one of the skills you start to hone in college through the process of meeting the requirements to get a degree. In addition to the technical skills you amass, planning and looking at the big picture seems to be incorporated into many classes you take. So, with my educational background, planning as well as thinking about and preparing for the future comes as second nature. Going through annual operational cycles also gives you a good feel for the future.

However, no matter how well you plan, as you have already seen, there are some things that can never be anticipated. In a service oriented business, people are a key factor in almost every plan, and you never really know how much you miss someone until they are a missing piece in an intricate plan. So begins the saga of a plan gone awry that turned into another fascinating adventure and another learning experience.

Let's step back for a moment, and take a look at the back-of-the-house operations and the fast-paced hustle and bustle of a large commercial kitchen. There are dozens and dozens of players on this stage, but for now let's focus on two key players. The first was Tony, the Executive Chef and the second was the Executive Sous Chef, Walter. In addition to being talented culinary artists, these two managers were in charge of every activity in the kitchen.

The Executive Chef is in charge of the overall management of the kitchen, while the Executive Sous Chef is the number two and takes on the responsibilities of the Executive Chef in his absence. Our Executive Sous Chef, Walter, was the key player in this incident, so let's take a closer look at how he figures into the picture. Walter had been with the hotel since the grand opening and had moved up to his current position based on hard work, steady performance, and personal growth in culinary and supervisory skills.

We had not originally included an Executive Sous Chef in our staffing pattern, but, after a couple of years, we discovered that extra management staffing was needed as our hotel became "the place" to hold meetings and banquets. Walter was the ideal candidate for this position when it was created; talented, hard working, supportive of the Executive Chef, and always smiling no matter how hectic things became.

He was perfect for the second-in-command position. Walter and Tony were a perfect team and Walter was happy with being number two. He was an easy-going "home town boy" who liked his job and had no apparent aspirations for the top position.

With that bit of background information, now comes the "twist" in our planning activities. As we planned for the coming months and reviewed the staffing pattern against the banquet schedule and occupancy levels, everything appeared to be in order. As anticipated, we were entering a slow period. We were planning, but the real focus of our attention in our plans had nothing to do with food preparation.

Everyone in the kitchen was talking about plans for the "big day." Walter and his fiancée, Georgette, were getting married! Careful plans had been made by the Executive Chef and I was fully supportive of everyone's efforts to clear the schedule for Walter to take off the last two weeks of June for their wedding and honeymoon.

Walter was so dedicated, that he had intentionally picked the last two weeks of June as this had been projected to be a slow period for banquets. In his absence, to maintain coverage and ensure quality, Tony had planned to spend extra time on the job.

Then, two days before the wedding, an unexpected event threw everyone's planning and careful preparation into question. Tony was unexpectedly hospitalized with acute tonsillitis. The GM and I discussed our options, and we agreed that asking Walter and Georgette to postpone their wedding plans was out of the question. There was no better time than now for Walter to be away, even if Tony might be out for a few days. I would just need to step in and fulfill Tony's essential duties to the best of my abilities.

Since our kitchen staff was experienced and knew what to do; I figured we would be able get along for a few days until Tony was able to return to work. That few days soon turned into a week, and then two weeks, as complications set in for Tony.

Fortunately, the Banquet Sous Chef was there to assist me. There were some small- to medium-sized functions of 25 to 100 guests and only two larger dinner functions for about 500 each scheduled during those weeks. This made my duties fairly straight forward; planning daily menu specials, approving purchase orders, preparing work schedules and opening and closing the kitchen.

During this time of need, I arrived at about 6:00 a.m. each morning and stayed until about 11:00 p.m. each evening. Although I was technically involved in all of the day-to-day activities, it was the staff that actually made sure that things ran smoothly. I worked alongside them making a few decisions and directing some activities in the kitchen, but mainly stayed out of their way unless asked a question or when needed to help during busy times. Among other things, I cracked eggs for an early morning breakfast for 100, trimmed meat to maintain our quality standards, and stepped in on "the line" providing needed breaks for the cooks.

There were some problems. None of the menu specials had been planned past Tuesday and purchase orders had not been completed for the coming weeks. The dish washing machine broke down in the middle of the dinner rush just as the dirty dishes from a banquet were arriving and the replacement part couldn't be delivered until the following day. All we could do was rinse the plates and tableware in the pot sinks and hold them in bus tubs for washing and sterilizing the next day.

We had to "86" (temporarily remove from the menu due to unavailability) some entrées when I misjudged demand and had been too conservative on some purchase orders. But, these types of problems were all manageable. The kitchen staff teased me and pulled a few good-natured tricks, but when all was said and done, we came through this challenge as a team and I had a tiring, but good, time in the process.

After two long weeks, Walter's return was the sweetest sight I had seen in what seemed like an eternity. When Tony returned the next day, it was almost Nirvana! What can we learn from these experiences?

- Planning helps you prepare for the future, but things don't always go as planned, so be prepared to make adjustments to your plans.
- Always plan, but be flexible when plans have to be changed, and make the needed change.
- No matter how high up you move in an organization or how important you think you are, remember you are still part of a team that needs everyone working together to be successful. When people are working hard, everyone appreciates it when you pitch in and help when needed.
- Don't wait for unplanned glitches to tap and appreciate the talents of your staff! Cross-train and develop employees not only to increase their own job satisfaction, but also to enhance their flexibility, knowledge, skills and abilities. The hotel business has always prided itself on preparing employees for job

growth and then rewarding them with promotion opportunities.
- Always be willing to listen to, observe, and recognize the value those with whom you work. They can either make your life easier or, if you ignore them, more difficult.

From then on, I had a new level of respect for, and from everyone on the kitchen staff. There was; however, another unusual incident that occurred during Tony and Walter's absences that is worth exploring. As you read the next chapter, and think about how you might have reacted in this situation.

30

The Fight

During Tony's and Walter's absences, there was one very exciting and extremely tense incident. The sequence of events that take place in this incident may have been the result of my youth, inexperience, stupidity, the absence of Tony and Walter or a combination of all four. After you finish reading all of the events that took place, I'll let you decide.

Let's set the stage before we begin looking at the events as they began to unfold. It was a very hot and humid June day in a very hot and humid kitchen. The hotel kitchen was big, in fact, very big with dozens of employees prepping, cooking, and cleaning up; in short, every activity needed to serve hundreds of restaurant and banquet guests.

With one large banquet taking place and servers darting in and out picking up orders as an expeditor checked plates and kept things moving on the line, it was a bit chaotic. Add in the clatter from the bussers dropping off bus tubs and the dishwashers loading and unloading the dish machine, it was not only hot and steamy, but also chaotic and noisy.

It seemed like every cooking device imaginable was in use that day and the heat they were generating all added to what seemed like an inferno. Everyone in the kitchen was dripping with sweat and you could feel the tensions mounting as the rapid-fire pace never seemed to abate.

It is important to note that when designing the hotel, the architects had decided there was no need to air condition the kitchen as this would have been an energy inefficient waste of money. Trying to cool down such a large space that was being heated by stoves, grills, fryers, broilers, boilers, ovens, and dish machines would have just been energy inefficient.

The only relief you could find from the heat was to catch a breeze from one of the two strategically placed fans at each end of the kitchen. However, there was no way to place a fan that would blow down "the line" as it would have interfered with the gas flames on these cooking surfaces.

With every cooking device in use and the dish machine spewing out a constant stream of steam, the environment had turned into one great big sauna. Anyone that had a chance to retrieve something from one of the walk-in coolers or freezers eagerly took advantage of the opportunity and probably even lingered for a few extra seconds.

It may have been inevitable, but it all happened so fast I'm not sure anyone noticed the unfolding events. One second, there was the hum of a finely tuned kitchen with everyone bearing the heat and getting orders out the door to the restaurant and plating for a pending banquet. The next second, there was total quiet with the exception of two employees screaming at the top of their lungs at each other.

From the best anyone could remember, it all started when a grill cook picked up a broiler cook's knife. There were several furious and exaggerated cuss words exchanged as the broiler cook, Mildred, grabbed her knife from the grill cook, Snake, and said; "If you every touch my *@!# knife again, I'll cut your *@!# heart out." Snake's reply was just as vitriolic. "If there's gonna to be any *@!# cutting, I'll be doing it."

Mildred brandished her knife and Snake broke off the top of a water glass next to his station. No, these names are not made up, and the scene was probably more chaotic and dramatic than you can even imagine. Why Snake even touched Mildred's knife, no one will ever know. In fact, if you know anything about a kitchen, you know that it is a grievous error of protocol to ever touch someone else's personal knife. Knives are very precious and extremely personal tools of the trade.

As they faced off, weapons at the ready, I could imagine an ensuing fight and blood all over the kitchen. So, in the heat of battle, I began stepping forward to get in between the two of them. As far as I was concerned, it was time for a little management intervention. It was time to get the combatants to cool down and talk things over. Enough was enough!

I had probably only taken three or four steps down the line toward the two screaming, cussing, spitting cooks when a pair of great big hands grabbed my shoulders and stopped me dead in my stride. These hands belonged to Louise, the sauté cook. She had an iron grasp on my shoulders and wouldn't let go.

Mildred and Snake were still screaming and flashing their weapons of choice at each other in wild-eyed sweeping motions. In the midst of this chaos, Louise said; "If they're going to do any cuttin', let them cut each other and not you. You can talk to them after they're finished with the cuttin'."

After what seemed like an eternity, Snake threw the jagged remains of the glass on the floor and stormed out of the kitchen. Then, just as soon as it had happened and everyone had frozen in their steps, it was over and the kitchen once again came humming back to life. No one said very much as a dishwasher came over and cleaned up the broken glass.

Then there were a lot of softly whispered comments. Mildred continued on with her work, fussing and cussing. One of the banquet cooks stepped in on the grill without even being asked and picked up Snake's duties just like nothing had ever happened while I stepped in to help out with plating the last of the banquet order. None of us spoke openly about the event for the rest of the shift.

When all of the banquets were plated and the dinner rush started to settle down, I went back to the kitchen office to write down the events of the day and gather my thoughts before they faded away from my memory.

As I was feverishly scribbling down notes, there was a knock on the door and Louise stuck in her head. All she said was; "We're glad you're still with us," and went back to her station. I'm glad I'm still here to tell this tale.

Snake never came back, not even to pick up his final check, but the story about the "young fool" who was going to break up the fight lingered on for a long time. What can we learn from this experience?

- Sometimes you find yourself in situations where you don't need to manage. At times, taking no action can be just as effective as taking action.
- Now some of you might be thinking, why didn't I terminate or suspend Mildred "pending investigation." Well, there is a saying that had been passed on to me by other foodservice managers and I heeded it in this situation. "Don't fire the dishwasher until the dishes are done." In this case, there was still a full night of cooking in front of us and she was a versatile and dependable cook who had been with the hotel for a long time, so there was no way I was going to "cut off my nose to spite my face."
- Disciplinary action was required, but mitigating circumstances also needed to be considered. Since this was the first incident, a serious written warning against this type of behavior was appropriate.

Luckily, by this time in my career I had worked closely enough with almost everyone in the kitchen and had gained their respect not only as a supervisor, but as a human being. With this experience behind us, let's take a look at a different kind of problem in the next chapter.

31

Sometimes it's not as Simple as You Think

Stephanie had completed a six-month training program in the sales office of the corporation's flagship hotel and was being placed in our hotel for her first permanent assignment. The notes that came along with her personnel file from the corporate Human Resources office looked promising.

Stephanie was a graduate of a well-known hospitality management program and she had successfully completed a three-month summer internship in the rooms division of a similar sized property of another hotel company prior to graduation.

Stephanie was being assigned to an open catering sales position in our hotel. The Director of Sales at our hotel, Jan, brought her by my office on the first day for introductions. As the Food and Beverage Director, I was excited about the prospect of having another person joining our selling efforts.

Any help we could get in filling our massive meeting space with food and beverage business was always welcomed. All of us on the senior management team were especially interested in the benefits of attracting more smaller group business to fill in gaps around our major convention group business.

After a brief discussion about her experiences it became obvious, that she had the personality and confidence to be a successful salesperson, but she didn't know very much about food and beverage operations. Other than a short stint as a waitress, the only knowledge she had about food and beverage operations came from her college courses, classroom projects and the six months of training she had gained in our flagship hotel. Jan didn't seem too concerned about this lack of practical experience as Stephanie had an outgoing personality and was eager to actively solicit new customers.

Who was I to be questioning people who had limited experience? I had found myself in many new situations with little or no practical experience and had been able to succeed, why couldn't she do the same. From her first week on the job, she proved that making cold calls on potential new customers came naturally.

Still a little concerned, I convinced Jan to at least let Stephanie work with the Banquet Manager on a few functions, both large and small, before she was "turned loose" on any more sales calls. We all agreed that this was a good idea and Stephanie spent the next week diligently shadowing Clarence while at the same time developing a list of prospects for sales calls during quiet times. She definitely showed a lot of motivation to learn and from all appearances, she was going to be a hard worker!

Stephanie was a hit with the banquet staff. Clarence said she was personable, listened well, followed directions and was always ready to pitch in. She seemed to have an innate sense of when to step in to make someone else's job easier, and she was a natural with the guests. When the week was over, we were all confident that Stephanie was ready to work the phones and "knock on doors" in search of new customers.

* * *

Stephanie must have been busy working the phones or making outside sales calls, because I didn't see her around the hotel for most of the following three weeks. Then one Friday afternoon she stopped by my office. She was beaming! The first thing out of her mouth was, "I made my first big sale today!"

She was right, it was a big sale! Her sales goals were to be focused on small groups of from 10 to 50 customers. This sale was for 250 and it was for a mid-week time slot for the next month during what looked like would be a very slow week. A last minute "fill-in" sale like this would really help in meeting our performance metrics.

Everything was sounding perfect, especially when she told me she didn't have to make any concessions to make the sale. Then just when I thought she had made the perfect sale; the operational "bomb shell" exploded. She told me what she had sold, and I moaned and slumped back in my chair.

An Accidental Hotelier

Stephanie informed me that she had sold a group of 250 women with a local philanthropic organization a menu that consisted of club sandwiches and apple pie á la mode. Just the thought of the logistics involved in this menu started my head to spin

It was like the two of us were in two entirely different worlds. Stephanie was glowing with the details of her sale and I had already started to panic. Could she have picked two more labor intensive and difficult items to prepare, plate and hold prior to serving; especially for a large and what would probably be a very demanding group? I didn't even want to think about the reaction from our chef when he heard about this menu!

The logistics would be a nightmare, but my mind couldn't seem to get away from thinking about the toast. It wasn't just the thought of crisping and holding 500 pieces of bacon and slicing 120+ tomatoes, or the thought of holding 250 pieces of apple pie in hot boxes and then scooping 250 servings of ice cream before they were rushed out of the door, it was the toast! We would need to make at least 750 pieces of toast, assemble the sandwiches and then get them sliced into those four nice little triangles in less than an hour, or there would be nothing but complaints about soggy entreés.

And as this thought was swirling through my mind, there stood a beaming Stephanie, basking in the glory of her sale. How could I break it to her that on paper this might look like a great sale, but from an operational perspective it would be a nightmare. For the kitchen, it would be a staffing and production problem, for our bottom line, it was a potential money losing proposition and for the group we would be serving, it could be a service quality disaster in the making. Rather than burst her bubble, I congratulated her and decided to talk with the Director of Sales and GM about how to turn this potential problem into a positive learning experience.

The GM's solution was brilliant and Jan whole-heartedly embraced his proposal. Rather than talk with Stephanie about labor costs, production difficulties, and hot box holding problems; let her experience them all. So, Stephanie and all the other members of the sales staff who would be in the office on the day of the function worked alongside the kitchen staff with the preparation and plating of this very special menu.

FYI

Actions like Stephanie selling club sandwiches and pie á la mode to a large group is a mistake that doesn't happen when a person starts gaining a little bit of operational experience. There are however, other decisions that are not mistakes, but just part of being in the business. Consider the customer who had his own farm and wanted to treat the dinner guests at his banquet to some of his fresh sweet corn. Everyone likes and tries to support the farm-to-fork concept, so how can you turn down a request like this? Sounds like fun, until 500 ears of corn arrive at the back loading dock at 3:00 p.m. that need to be cleaned, cooked and plated for a 7:00 p.m. banquet. With that time frame, a whole lot of us got to enjoy some shucking and de-silking!

Stephanie and her colleagues were not as enthusiastic about this project as Jan, but they all agreed to pitch in and help. With everyone's help, the event was a success. But, even more important, after this learning experience, Stephanie went back to another customer who had already booked a function and convinced them to change their menu. If she hadn't, we would have been making 125 pineapple boats filled with tuna salad for another women's group.

Like you have already read in many other incidents, we always grow when we learn from what could be considered mistakes or errors in judgment and there is much to be learned from this experience.

- Delivering a quality foodservice experience requires an intricate balance of rhythm, timing, and flow. If any of these get out of balance, service and customer satisfaction will suffer.
- Some things may look good on paper, but they aren't as simple to accomplish as they appear on paper or as described in textbooks. Search for solutions rather than placing blame and turn problems into learning experiences.

- Teamwork is important in every organization, but it is mandatory for successful hotel operations. A little teamwork can make a major task a manageable feat. And, all's well that ends well!

In the next chapter you will discover how important the "entire team" is to successful hotel operations.

32

When it Snows in the South

From previous episodes, you have already learned how important planning can be. So, when the alarm went off at 5:00 a.m., there was no hitting the snooze button. It was going to be a busy day, and I wanted to be at the hotel early this particular morning, no later than 6:00 a.m.

The hotel had been full all week, and several more days of full houses were still on the books as a large convention group was in-house and another was scheduled in right in back of it. Even though I was confident in my staff, I still wanted to be there to help out where needed and provide moral support if nothing else.

Rubbing my eyes and looking out the window, I could only stare in disbelief and my mind began to race. It was snowing and the parking lot in front of my apartment was already covered with at least four inches of the fluffy white stuff. If I had still been living up North, where snow was common, this would not have been a problem, but a thick layer of "white stuff" here in the South was problematic. People down here were not used to seeing snow, and they just don't know how to handle snow; especially when it comes to driving in it.

Would I even be able to get to work? How many of our employees would brave the elements and even try to get to work? Would the city buses be running? Would the airport be open? Would our current guests check out, and what if they didn't and more arrived? This and many more questions ran through my mind as I turned on the radio hoping to get a weather and traffic update.

The drive to the hotel that morning was a little nerve-racking, but I made it with a little slipping and sliding. The trickiest part was negotiating the hill leading down from my apartment. I just held my breath, eased my car over to the curb at the top of the hill and skidded down all the way through the stop sign at the bottom of the hill. From there on the drive wasn't that tricky as the roads were still empty of traffic. Rather than taking the Interstate, I slowly eased my way into town on the back roads.

While gingerly creeping through the snow-packed streets, avoiding all of the main roads and listening to the radio, I couldn't help but groan. All the schools had been closed and the city buses would not be running today, and to make matters even worse, unseasonably cold weather was still in the forecast for at least the next two days. Everyone was being encouraged to stay home, unless it was an emergency, and several accidents had already been reported. During my time of working up North, I had learned to negotiate icy and snowy roads, and I had left early enough that there was almost no one on the roads.

When I arrived at the hotel, I was relieved to see that the GM was already there and that some of the kitchen staff were too. The night auditors had already talked the situation over with the GM and had agreed to stay a few extra hours, especially since it didn't make any sense for them to try to leave anytime soon.

Several other employees arrived after braving the slick streets and sidewalks, but the calls were starting to come in from many more employees who would not be able to get to work as bus service was shut down until further notice. When the restaurant manager arrived, he brought even more bad news; the streets were now almost impassable due to the number of "fender benders" and stalled cars.

By 7:00 a.m., the hotel was coming to life. The lobby was beginning to fill with guests talking about the weather and discussing travel options, and a line was forming in front of the restaurant. It was past opening time, but we still couldn't open. There just wasn't enough staff to serve our guests. Desperate times like this, call for desperate measures, and improvisation became the "modus operandi" for the day. The GM stepped in and began visiting with the guests in the lobby about their travel dilemmas and as I headed to the restaurant, he asked me to get a couple of big coffee servers and paper cups up to the lobby as soon as possible.

When I arrived at the restaurant, the manager had already decided that with only three other employees there was no way to operate with our typical table service routine. There would be no way to establish a consistent pattern of "rhythm, timing, and flow" today! He and his "skeleton crew" were putting together two eight-foot tables they had grabbed from the banquet area for buffet service. The kitchen staff was already pulling out large sheet pans full of bacon from the ovens and the only dishwasher who had made it into work was cracking eggs in preparation for mass scrambling. We would be serving a very, very limited menu, but there would be plenty of hot food and lots of coffee.

The other big problem we were facing was the seated breakfast that had been scheduled for the ballroom. There was no way we would have the banquet staff needed to serve these guests in that setting, so they were directed to either the lobby for a cup of coffee or the restaurant to a true "help yourself buffet" with an apology and a request to, "please be understanding" and help us through this emergency.

To be sure there was a long line at the restaurant, but no one seemed all that impatient as there really was no other place to go. Everyone was cooperative, no one lingered at their seats as they knew others were waiting for their table, and in a couple of hours there was no longer a line. We even asked guests if they could help out by bussing their own tables, and most of them were more than happy to lend a helping hand!

The GM put together a quick letter explaining the circumstances and had copies placed at the front desk and under each door. Because of the snow emergency there would only be very limited housekeeping services that day. What started out as an emergency, if not a service disaster, soon turned into a time of adventure and cooperation for everyone.

As the day wore on, a few more employees straggled in and we began to feel like we would all survive. We had to modify all of the menus in the restaurant and banquets to limited-service buffets, but almost everyone seemed to recognize the problems and did their part to adjust and help. To be honest, there were some guests we just couldn't please, but the GM handled these situations.

This was far from a typical day in the life of a hotelier, but by now, I had learned to expect the unexpected. Maybe I shouldn't have been surprised, but I was amazed at how well the few employees who arrived that day, worked as a team. They just instinctively knew what to do and where they were needed. Nobody worried about job descriptions, they all just got the job done and made sure that our guests had what they needed.

I don't want to make it all sound rosy; we did have a handful of angry customers. Some were insulted by the idea, if not the request, to bus their own tables. Others couldn't understand why they didn't have full housekeeping services, why they couldn't get room service, and why the only food available was buffet style. It was a good thing for us the hotel's hot water system didn't fail on this day!

The biggest problems we faced were the late check-outs as some guests were not able to leave that afternoon and then there was the difficulty of getting those rooms ready for our new guests who began straggling in. We did not get everyone into their rooms until very late that night. However, a situation that could have been a disaster ended up being an adventure that turned into another learning experience.

- Improvise when necessary. There was one silver lining to this weather problem. We opened the lounge early, with limited service, and did a brisk business. Stranded hotel guests are just like stranded airline passengers, they like to drink!

- Solving problems, meeting guest needs, training and cross-training employees are all part of every manager's and supervisor's responsibilities in a hotel. Knowing that there will always be unexpected problems keeps the job from being anything but dull.

- Guests can be amazingly understanding, especially when you clearly communicate the details of the problem and what you are doing to correct it. If you demonstrate confidence and have fun in the midst of a problem others can join in, creating a positive experience.

- When you treat employees as team members, they will work as team members, despite job classifications, when the need arises.

As you will see in the next episode, having dignitaries in your hotel can lead to some unexpected excitement.

33

Don't Mess Around with Security

Being one of the few premier hotels in a large urban area, we were very accustomed to dealing with a host of very important people (VIPs) from celebrities to dignitaries. The list of politicians, movie stars, athletes, coaches and sports teams, performers and comedians we dealt with on a regular basis would fill pages.

Many were difficult to accommodate and often very demanding, but they were always willing to pay top dollar to ensure their demands were met. We dealt with so many special guests, and their entourages that after a while, it became almost normal for us to have another VIP speaking to a group or staying in the hotel. In passing, we would often ask each other; "Do we have anybody special in the house this week?"

One particular VIP was scheduled for a noon speaking engagement following a particularly busy two week period of full houses and back-to-back maximum capacity banquets. My counterpart, Beau, with whom I usually shared manager-on-duty chores in the evenings and on weekends had been on vacation, so I had been putting in some extraordinarily long hours. During Beau's absence, key members of the management team had a meeting with the Secret Service, as this particular VIP was contemplating running for President of the United States.

Our meeting with the Secret Service agents was straightforward as all of us had already received security clearances for previous political visitors. We discussed logistics for the visit and the fund-raising banquet where the keynote address was to be delivered. The only thing that was different with this visit was the fact that there had been a death threat against this particular candidate, so security measures would be increased.

Prior to his arrival, Secret Service agents would be starting at the top of the hotel and working their way down as they passed through every nook and cranny, securing all public areas, mechanical areas, and access points to back-of-the-house service areas. Once they had "swept" an area, a security seal was placed on the door.

If the seal were broken, then that area would have to be re-secured. Our responsibility was to have a member of our management staff accompany each Secret Service agent when the "sweep" was made and then to clearly instruct every member of our staff not to enter any of the doors that had been secured. These seemed like simple enough instructions.

Beau returned from vacation the morning of the speech, rested and ready to go to work. I came in to meet him that morning and do a quick briefing before taking a couple of days off. Mostly we talked about his vacation. In passing, I told him who was coming in for the speech and that he, Beau, had already been cleared by the Secret Service. I was tired, and ready to go home, so forgot to tell him a couple of very important details.

The first important detail I forgot to pass along, was about the security seals that had been placed on the doors once an area had been cleared and secured by the Secret Service. The second important detail I forgot to pass along, was that because of the death threats, sharp-shooters had been placed on roofs of our building and the two high rise buildings that were in the line-of-sight of the hotel.

Shortly after I left, an alarming call came in to the hotel and was passed on to Beau. The concerned caller reported that there was a man on top of the building across the street from our hotel with a rifle. Beau didn't just go to one of the upper floors and look out the window. Being a "take charge" type of guy and also being both curious and concerned, he rushed up to the top of the hotel, opened the roof access door and stepped outside to get a better look.

The roof door had already been secured! Now as Beau would later tell the story, when he opened the door, he came face-to-face with a Secret Service agent pointing a rifle in his direction. In not very friendly terms, he was told to lie down on the roof, face down, and put his hands behind his head. At first he was just terrified. There he was, laying on the roof trying to explain why he was on the roof to a guy who didn't believe his story and didn't really care.

Because of my lack of clear communications, in his rush to get to the roof, Beau made two very serious mistakes. First, he broke through a security sealed door and second, he was not wearing his Secret Security clearance pin. In all honesty, in my rush to get home, I may have forgotten to tell him about the security clearance pin which was in his top desk drawer and the need to wear it at all times while on property that day. So there he was, stuck on the roof with a rifle pointed at his head from 9:00 a. m. to 1:30 p. m. Needless to say, Beau has never forgiven me for my communication oversights!

Other than this being a harrowing experience for Beau, is there anything to be learned from this incident? Without a doubt, the answer is yes.

- Fatigue can lead to poor communications, judgment calls and decisions. Since the hotel business often demands that you put in long hours, at times, don't forget to take care of yourself physically and get the rest you need to stay focused.
- Pay attention to details and be a clear communicator. When you are verbally communicating complicated or critical information to someone, make sure they understand what you have said as a lot can be lost in the transmission of information.
- Make sure the person to whom you are trying to communicate with understands what you have said by having them repeat back to you what you are attempting to communicate.
- For each security event, have staff read and sign a statement that they understand and will uphold all

security measures (this may need to be written in several different languages). Intentional or not, don't interfere in matters of security, especially when it involves the Secret Service.

As you turn the page to the next chapter we'll take a look at not guests in general, but a situation involving a guest who thought she was very special and demanded very special treatment because of who she was.

34

Wait Until You Hear From My Daddy!

Establishing and having your performance measured against metrics is a way of life in the hotel business. Meeting and hopefully exceeding these standards becomes both an individual and team challenge and cause for celebration on a daily, weekly and monthly basis. There are also times of discouragement, and adjustments, when they are not being met. With that in mind, we were just finishing up what had been a really good week.

The hotel had been full or nearly full the entire week with a really strong average daily rate and in addition to packed banquet functions, the groups in house had been big spenders in all of our food and beverage outlets. We were not only meeting all of our performance targets, but we were also exceeding every one of them. With performance like this, there was no doubt that we were going to close out the week and month on a financial "high note."

In order to achieve our goals, especially in food and beverage operations, meeting and exceeding the demands of meeting planners was especially important. This week, one particularly important, "blue chip" client who booked numerous room nights and functions throughout the year and never seemed to be particularly price sensitive had been in the hotel since Tuesday afternoon.

This particular client was so important to our business that I had requested to be scheduled as the manager on duty on the evening shift over the weekend to be present and make sure everyone was completely satisfied with every detail during their stay. And, everything was going along as planned; her meeting had been perfect. That's the way things seem to go in the hotel business. When things go well, they seem to go very well and when things go wrong, they can quickly spiral out of control and go really wrong!

FYI

Creating the perfect environment for celebrating weddings, birthdays, anniversaries and other special occasions is just part of the job, or maybe it's a passion for perfection. Standing on the sidelines and witnessing the excitement and joy of the honorees and guests is an incredibly satisfying experience; just knowing that you and your team made everything perfect for the special occasion should be thanks enough. However, the thank yous, hugs and hard-pumping handshakes accompanying the end of the event just energize you to try even harder the next time!

I was basking in the glory of our success and had no way of knowing that the situation I was walking into was going to be a bad one, when I got the call to come down to the lounge. The lead bartender met me at the bottom of the staircase and briefed me on what to expect before we got to the lounge. As I mentioned before, our lounge was high-energy with top flight bands and dancing six nights a week. It was known as the best "hook-up spot" in town and it was definitely the place to "see" and "be seen."

It was early Sunday evening, and things were usually quiet on Sundays, as there was no live music. Even though this was typically a slow night, the lounge was still busy, as the hotel was almost full. The problem I was walking into was a situation involving one of our guests (she was charging her drinks to her hotel room). The guest in question was a young lady who had been drinking all afternoon and was now clearly intoxicated and had become obnoxious. It was her twenty-first birthday, and she was letting everyone within ear shot know that she was taking advantage of her legal right to drink.

Enjoying yourself and having a good time celebrating is one thing, but becoming intoxicated and obnoxious with other guests and employees is another thing. The servers and bartenders should probably have "cut her off earlier," but as they said, "She was pacing herself and just seemed to be having a good time." Now, her personality had changed, and she was demanding to be served and cussing out everyone in sight about being refused service, and refusing to "settle down" with a cup of coffee or leave and go to her room.

In her rage, she was claiming that she would get everyone in the lounge fired since her Daddy, "owned the hotel." With a claim like this, being cautious was a good idea. There was always a possibility that her father may have been an "owner" as there were several large investors in this property, just like almost every other hotel property. Not many hotels actually own the physical properties, but operate the properties under management contracts.

As the manager on duty, it was normal practice to step in and try to diffuse situations like this. Customers typically responded positively when they were dealing with someone they perceived as having authority. I prided myself on having a reputation as being pretty good at dealing with disgruntled guests, but I was getting nowhere with this lady. She kept screaming the same thing over and over as I continued to try to calm her down, "You get me a drink, or my Daddy will get you fired!"

Finally after taking several minutes of her verbal abuse, I told her that unless she settled down immediately, I would have security remove her from the lounge. All of my attempts at appeasing her had been going nowhere, but the threat of security did the trick. This was just a bluff on my part as we only needed security to be present Monday through Saturday during closing time. As she stomped off in a huff, her parting and "slurry words" were, "Wait until you hear from my Daddy, you'll be fired!" To my relief, the immediate problem was solved, but her threat did weigh on my mind making for a restless night.

Her threat did come true when I got THE CALL from her Daddy on Monday morning. Yes, he was, in fact, one of the investors in the hotel and he had reserved a room for his daughter and given her and "open-ended" account to celebrate her birthday. Based on what his daughter had told him, he was furious. According to her, everyone on the hotel staff had been rude (especially me), failed in our service delivery and by our actions had thoughtlessly ruined her special day. He demanded an immediate apology and, like his daughter thought that I should be fired for my unprofessionalism, or at the very least, be disciplined. He informed me in no uncertain terms that he would be meeting with the GM before the day was over!

After he had finished venting and it was painful to be on the receiving end of his "tongue-lashing," as calmly as I could, I told him my version of the events of the evening in question. Then, there was a long pause, a very long pause, and to my surprise, all he said was, "Everything is copacetic" and hung up. I wasn't really sure what had just taken place on the phone call or what this word, copacetic, meant, until I was able to look up its meaning. Copacetic is an interesting word, one I had never heard used before, and at the time it sounded a little scary.

If you don't know the meaning of the word, copacetic, look it up before you read any further. If you had to look up the meaning or already know the meaning of this word, then the following comments about what can be learned from this incident will make sense to you.

- Setting difficult to achieve, but achievable goals can serve as powerful individual and team motivators. Reporting on performance and being measured against these goals can be both gratifying when they are met and/or exceeded, and humbling when they are missed.
- Just like the Golden Rule, treat every guest the way that you would like to be treated in a similar situation. There is nothing wrong with being firm when dealing with problem guests. You never know what has been going on in their lives, and "venting" their anger and frustrations at service employees is one of the realities of being of service in the hotel business.
- Always inform your superiors of potential problems so that they can be forewarned and prepared to deal with them.
- Owners are important, even though you may never know who they are, but they should never knowingly be treated differently than any other guest. Although it may be tempting to treat an owner, or even corporate executives differently, think of every guest as an "owner," and you will always deliver, "knock your socks off customer service!"

As you turn the page to the next chapter we'll take a look at not guests in general, but a situation involving a very special guest who demanded and paid for extra special attention.

35

Confidentiality Counts!

Right from the start, as was obvious from the attention that was being given to every detail, you could tell this was going to be a very special guest. I had previously dealt with Presidential candidates, ambassadors, foreign dignitaries, Senators, Governors, and a host of other dignitaries. Along the way, I had been cleared by the Secret Service to deal with some of these high profile guests. But, this guest was different. He had his own security force, and the director of his force was not impressed with my Secret Service clearance. His team would perform their own background checks, or at least, that's what we were told.

Let's backtrack a moment and begin with the previously calendared request to schedule the first meeting. The GM had requested a meeting with me and a "guest." There was no name and no hints as to what the meeting would be about. I asked him about this meeting several times in the days before the scheduled appointment and all he would say was, "No big deal, nothing for which you need to plan."

On the day of the meeting I showed up at the GM's office about fifteen minutes ahead of time as usual. The door was closed, and after knocking and entering, to my surprise, the meeting was already underway, but there were two guests rather than one. There were no introductions, just a nod of the head and a motion for me to come in. After a short silence, one of the guests asked my GM, "Are you sure we can trust him?"

The GM nodded his head in the affirmative, and I was asked to close the door before the conversation resumed. Needless to say, they had my attention and had piqued my curiosity. What was this meeting all about?

I quickly learned that they had not uncovered any problems in their background checks on me. Their only question was, "Could I hold in strictest confidence the name and details of the arrival, stay, and departure of a very special guest?" With my "yes" answer, the meeting continued. It was well over an hour into the meeting before the name of this special guest was revealed.

Here were the basic details of the planned visit. Our special guest would rent the top two floors of the hotel, the night before his arrival and the night of his stay. He would occupy the Presidential Suite at one end of the top floor and his security detail would occupy two rooms at the opposite end of the floor-by the elevators. The floor below, would remain unoccupied and was to be sealed-off. The elevators also were to be locked so that no one would have access to either of the top two floors.

An Accidental Hotelier

Everyone had already been informed that these two floors were being blocked off for two days to complete some basic maintenance and scheduled upgrades. However, since purchasing had not placed any orders for any new furniture, fixtures, or soft goods and no maintenance activities had been scheduled with the maintenance department, there was already a little gossip around the hotel about what might be happening, but the grapevine was devoid of any credible rumors. Our special guest did not want anyone to know that he would be staying in our hotel. In fact, reservations had been made under his name at a competing hotel that was closer to the convention center. It seemed like no detail had been left untouched.

Although I was the Food and Beverage Director, several of my planned duties for this visit had nothing to do with food and beverage. My first job, planned for his arrival, had something to do with garbage. His arrival had been timed to coincide with the afternoon garbage pickup. His car, complete with security guards, would pull in at the back loading dock just ahead of our daily scheduled garbage pickup.

He would hop out, come in through the back service door where I would be holding the service elevator. I would place an "out of service" sign on the elevator prior to his arrival, making sure that it was ready to immediately whisk him to the top floor. All of this was timed to the garbage truck emptying the dumpster and blocking the view of the loading dock and back door. We would put the service elevator "out of order" again for both his departure from the hotel and return to the hotel that evening after his performance.

Everything went as planned. Mission accomplished! There were several "groupies" and photographers hanging around the front entrance of the hotel, but they never became aware of our clandestine activities.

In our brief elevator rides, I discovered that our special guest was engaging, charming, and genuinely interested in a little bit of small talk. We were just talking with each other like he was no one special.

My other service obligation during this visit was food and beverage related. I was to be prepared to cook for our special guest at any time during his stay. He would be paying extra to keep the kitchen "hot" all night and preparing everything on the dining room menu as well as any special request would be considered to be a reasonable request.

On the evening of our special guest's stay, the kitchen staff was surprised when I told them not to turn anything off at the end of the shift. The grapevine had still not picked up on what was going on. My excuse for keeping the kitchen hot, was that I wanted to perform some temperature and maintenance checks on our equipment when it wouldn't be disruptive to daily operations. Even though the Executive Chef offered to stay and help, I told him that he had been working some long hours, "So take the night off. This job only requires one of us."

We typically closed the kitchen sometime between 10:30 p. m. and 11:00 p. m. and I had a long wait until I finally got the "much anticipated" call at 2:00 a. m. Would the order be for a thick juicy steak, salad and baked potato; chicken cordon bleu with asparagus and hollandaise sauce; Chateaubriand and cherries jubilee; or maybe shrimp scampi? I was tense with anticipation, but ready for anything. Would the request be for one person or more? When the call came, it was for a cheeseburger, well done, with carrot sticks. Well, so much for the opportunity to showcase my culinary skills.

Why all the secrecy? The media reported that there had been throngs of groupies at every major hotel that evening trying to catch a glimpse of our visiting star. We pulled it off, no one knew he was staying at our hotel and he had a peaceful and relaxing visit on at least one stop on his tour schedule.

When it was all over and the secret became known: the females on our staff were angry that the visit had been kept a secret. Even my wife was angry that I had kept the visit a secret. It was truly an honor to have been entrusted with providing this special level of service! Was there more to this encounter other than learning how much planning and coordination it takes to serve a star? The answer is yes, there is a great deal to be learned.

- Orchestrating details for celebrity stays requires a great deal of planning, coordination, and at times secrecy. When a hotel gains a reputation for success in these efforts, additional business will follow.
- Confidentiality, an important part of the service contract, can create business opportunities and positively impact profitability.
- People can keep a secret, and having a "clean" background can create unexpected opportunities for personal growth.

- Keep your personal life out of the social media, and only do and share those things that you wouldn't mind having publicized. This point is so important, that it bears repeating again. Don't post anything on social media sites that might be viewed negatively in the future!
- Unlike some other famous people I had served, this special guest was gracious and neither demanding nor demeaning.

If there hadn't already been enough excitement, the events in the next chapter will prove that history repeats itself.

36

The Union Knocks Again

By law, union representatives must wait for at least one year after a failed National Labor Relations sanctioned representation election, before attempting further organizing activities; otherwise the union would be guilty of committing an unfair labor practice. So, it came as no surprise when the first signs of organizing activities appeared just one year and one day after the first election.

This wasn't the start of the campaign, but the union was "testing the waters" for launching a full-blown campaign. Within weeks, after a campaign could be legally restarted, we knew that we were headed for another organizing campaign. The only question was when? We had a while to wait, but a few months later we were in the midst of a full-blown organizing campaign. Having been through this process before, no one on the management team was looking forward to the tensions that lay ahead.

The union was much more aggressive in this campaign and had identified employees that they thought would be good shop stewards if they prevailed in their attempts to unionize the hotel. In fact, one of the most outspoken employees in favor of the union worked on the evening shift in the restaurant. The turmoil we had experienced with changes in the food and beverage departments had us focusing most of our attention in these areas. As the campaign progressed, it became obvious that things would be much more acrimonious than any of us had imagined.

When election-day finally arrived and the results were announced, the union had prevailed and won the right to represent the employees in the bargaining group by one vote. The results were just the reverse of the previous election. There were some smirks and taunting remarks by some of the employees, but mostly there was dejection and the obvious feeling of defeat by many of the managers and supervisors who felt hurt, anger and betrayal at the result.

Always a model of self-control, the GM, however, was even more resigned and explained that management would need to learn to work with the union while keeping our guests as our number one priority. But first, before conceding the outcome, our lawyers wanted to explore having the result overthrown by pursuing several potentially unfair labor practice actions on the part of the union.

Although we held out hope that the election results would be overturned, ultimately, each of these potential unfair labor practice violations were resolved in the union's favor, and the first bargaining session was scheduled. This time, since I was so deeply involved in operations, I was not asked to participate in negotiations, but was asked to continue doing my job while attempting to maintain labor-management harmony.

Those of us on the senior management team that were not participating in the negotiation process, received updates after each session, but each update was the same. All the union representatives seemed to want was a "dues check-off" (a contract provision that requires the employer to deduct union dues, assessments, and initiation fees from the pay of all members of the bargaining unit). The hotel's primary concerns were in the area of management rights (a contract clause that defines those activities that management can undertake without the consent of the union).

After many preliminary bargaining sessions, just to get the negotiation process moving forward, the management team offered a package with expanded management prerogatives and a small cut in wages to some positions, increases in others and some limits to benefits. To everyone's surprise, the union negotiating team indicated that they thought they could get the contract ratified by the rank-and-file if we would include the check-off provision.

As tempting as this offer might have seemed, there was no way that our management team would have taken advantage of our employees by agreeing to this type of unbalanced package. This is not how you build employee loyalty, trust or good working relationships. What this action did reveal was the fact that the union had depleted its resources for organizing other hotels in the city and desperately needed to replenish its cash reserves.

With this realization, management was in no hurry to move forward and the negotiations lingered on for months. When a contract was finally presented to the rank-and-file for ratification, it was no different than what the employees had been receiving before the election with the exception of a grievance procedure and a dues check-off provision.

It wasn't long after the contract was ratified that one the employees who had been so involved in the campaign for the union and the negotiations confided in me that our focus on what we thought was the most important employee group had been misdirected. The only reason many employees voted for the union was that management had done nothing to protect the employees in housekeeping who were being unfairly dealt with by their supervisor.

Another-piece of enlightening information was that one of the original restaurant servers who opened the hotel and had been very quiet from outward appearances during the campaign was now a shop steward. As she told me later, everyone in her family belonged to a union, and she wanted to have that same sense of belonging.

The sad news, from a management perspective, was that it was our own fault that the union had won. Then, when the employees looked at what they had "gained," some started talking to us about how to start a union de-certification campaign. There is much to be learned from this episode.

- People, especially employees, like the feeling of belonging to identifiable groups, and unions can meet this need by providing a sense of security and identity.

This same sense of belonging and group identification can also be provided by the hotel. One way or another, employees will strive to have this need met.

- Employees expect to be protected and treated fairly by management. If management fails in these tasks, they may seek outside help which is one of the appeals of being protected by a union.
- Nurture positive labor relationships and monitor and respond to labor dissatisfaction. Don't allow "us versus them" movements to take root; deal with problems before they fester. Always work to keep employees feeling like they are an important and integral part of the team.
- Keep lines of communication open so that small problems can be managed before they grow like a cancer and become big problems. Provide a means for employees to anonymously share grievances – from old fashioned employee suggestion boxes to electronic "tip hotlines."
- A union is just like any other business, it needs a stream of cash flow to fulfill its mission and a dues check-off provision provides that stream.

The final episode in this book is not related in any way to losing the campaign and the eventual unionization of the hotel, although it may appear that way. Hopefully, appearances are deceiving, as the events in the next chapter are incredibly upbeat following what could be considered a downbeat chapter.

37

The Reward

Just as it did for me, your journey toward becoming a hotelier will offer you a challenging, if not, adventure-filled career. You can expect not only, to work hard and put in some long hours, but you can also expect to experience a great deal of personal satisfaction and at times unexpected rewards.

As emotions were beginning to settle down after a labor contract had been signed, and I was beginning to cut back on my hours and once again begin enjoying some of the local pleasures, I got a call from the VP of Food and Beverage. With the whole-hearted support of my GM, he was asking me if I would be interested in joining a week-long food and beverage training event.

When he described everything that was being planned for the week and then said it would be in Florida in March, I couldn't resist. Do you remember that hotel feasibility study I worked on during my early days in the corporate office? Well, this event was being held at that same hotel.

One of the fringe benefits of this event was that we all got to bring our significant others. When I arrived at our destination hotel, I was looking for some other Food and Beverage Directors, but to my surprise, I was the only one there; everyone else who was attending was a chef. I already knew some to the chefs as I had been in their hotels on those early internal auditing adventures. So, it was fun to catch-up with each other and to do a little reminiscing.

After a casual pool-side welcoming reception on Sunday evening, we began our training on Monday morning, and before we even got started, I had a big surprise! My surprise was that I was being bestowed the title of "honorary chef" and being invited, as an equal, to participate in all of the activities based on my "unconventional" learning experiences in the kitchen during Tony's and Walter's absences.

The training sessions were phenomenal, and I can never describe how much I learned. Every day, each one of the Chefs showed off a new technique or time-saving trick from which we all benefited.

But, the crowning glory for this training event was an invitation from Disney World to tour their back-of-the-house operations and work with their Executive Chef with their culinary staff serving as our guides and hosts. If that wasn't enough after a morning of learning and sharing, we were all, spouses and significant others, treated to a gourmet lunch that had been especially designed to showcase the best of Disney's foodservice creativity.

Then, just when we thought it couldn't get any better, the VP for Human Resources of Disney World who had been with us all day, gave us VIP passes to the park. We never had to wait in line for any of the rides, giving us the opportunity to enjoy most of the entire park in one afternoon. What a reward and what an experience!

This experience shows, once again, that dedication and hard work do pay off. I still enjoy planning menus, cooking, showing off some of the unique "garde manger" techniques I learned during those training sessions whenever I have the opportunity to entertain.

Each of these situations, many of them testing my abilities and lack of experience, provided learning opportunities worthy of being shared as they prepared me for career growth and satisfaction on the path to becoming a hotelier. There are many more stories that could be shared, but by now you should have fairly good insights into an exciting world called the hotel business.

My hope is that you learn from the experiences presented and decide to follow in my footsteps, not as an accidental hotelier, but as an intentional hotelier!

- Take advantage of every situation that provides an opportunity for you to learn and grow professionally. They are often presented in unusual ways.
- Hard work and dedication will be recognized and rewarded. If your hard work is not recognized, find an organization that will honor your efforts.

- Finally, if you can't learn from your experiences, you will never grow professionally. Learn, grow, and enjoy the business!

Just for the fun of it, take a look at the next chapter and discover if you have already developed or are developing some of the common characteristics of successful hoteliers.

Common Habits of Successful Hoteliers

When this journey began, I had no intention of starting down the path to becoming a hotelier. However, after a few short years, marked by an incredible supporting cast of mentors, and being surrounded by a team of dedicated employees focused on providing exceptional customer service, I was well on my way to wanting to be a long-term part of this industry. Combining an innate desire to serve others with a number of unforgettable adventures, challenges, and a wide variety of on-the-job learning opportunities, made me realize that it was more than just a job or a career, I had become hopelessly addicted to the hotel business.

To this day as I deal with people in any type of setting, I am often asked, why I demonstrate such a strong desire to serve. My answer is always the same, the desire to serve has been engrained in me by my experiences in the hotel business. It is a business that teaches you the importance of always focusing your attention on serving the needs of others.

When looked at through the eyes of a hotelier, it becomes second nature to recognize situations involving satisfied and even truly delighted guests. You also quickly recognize the people who are serving them. From several years of being around both guests and service providers, I have become keenly aware of the best practices that make positive service encounters in a hotel setting possible. After further study, it became obvious not only in my own thought processes and actions, but also in those same actions of others I have had the opportunity to work with and observe, that there are certain habits all successful hoteliers have in common. They may not even be aware of these habits as they seem to develop either consciously or subconsciously over time as they become immersed in their careers.

Not all of these habits will be developed all at once. Different habits will manifest themselves at different stages of your career, especially as you begin to observe and model the behaviors of other successful managers and gain experience in different aspects of a well-managed property. Several of the more common habits of successful hoteliers are described below.

As you read each one, think about it and notice if some or all of them may be reflective of your own thoughts and behaviors. Ask yourself, do any of these habits describe me? If you read them, and chuckle to yourself, that they do in fact resemble how you look at the service world, it is a sure sign that you are probably becoming the definition of a true hotelier and may have already become addicted to the business. Although these common habits are listed in no particular order, let's start with one "telltale" habit that will quickly develop in your hotel career and then move on to other common habits.

Number One. *Pride in ownership*. When walking your property, you pay meticulous attention to even the smallest details. In the process you exude an indescribable "pride of ownership" as this is your "house!" You want every guest who enters your doors to see and experience the best you have to offer. While visiting anyone else's property, you can't help but benchmark your property against their property, making mental notes of how your property and staff compares. Other little things like your first impressions when walking into a guest room are tell-tale signs of being a hotelier. The feeling that you are the first person that has ever entered the room makes you think; a job well done on the part of the staff.

Number Two. *A never ending obsession for attention to details*. There are several indicators of a hotelier's keenly developed sense of attention to details. No matter where you are in a hotel, you always find yourself looking around to see if there are burned out light bulbs in need of replacement in lobby, hallways and meeting room light fixtures. You may even notice that you have become compulsive about this; immediately scanning and counting the number of light bulbs that have burned out when you walk into the public areas of any building. You have also developed a compulsive habit of picking up stray scraps of paper, cigarette butts and other pieces of trash found anywhere on your property. Conversely, when you notice that all of the light bulbs are working and there is not even one stray piece of trash on a property, you make a mental note that the property is well-run with a management staff that also has an eye on details.

Number Three. *A habit of "walking" your property at least one a day if not more often.* It is more than just management by walking around, your innate curiosity or your focus on paying attention to details. You want to see your property through the eyes of your guests, meet and greet your guests and always be present for your staff. When walking through the guestroom hallways of your property or as a guest in another property, one of your criterion for measuring the efficiency and effectiveness of food and beverage operations is noticing the presence or absence of room service trays. You may even find yourself lying down on a guest room bed during an inspection, thinking about what your guests will see.

Number Four. *Selecting a seat in a restaurant.* When being seated in a restaurant, you always ask to be seated at a table where you can see the service areas, ordering systems, cash register, kitchen and front door. You never seem to be completely comfortable during the dining experience unless everything appears to be moving smoothly and guests are being served and cared for attentively. One of the little things you can't help but notice, and it may have even become an obsession, is when and how water glasses are being refilled during the course of a meal. Any time a water glass sits half empty for more than a few minutes, you get a little fidgety and your eyes start darting around looking for someone on the service staff who will also notice and take care of the customer; all of the time wondering why it seems like no one in the restaurant is paying any attention to the needs of the guests.

Number Five. *A strong desire to step in and solve customer service problems.* When checking into a hotel (you still check in manually and not electronically) and a line has formed at the front desk; you start to wonder if something has failed with the technology, there is a trainee on the desk or perhaps someone misjudged the staffing needs for that particular time period. You feel the same type of impulses when dining and have the desire to start pouring coffee or visiting with guests when service failures are obvious and not being addressed. Customer service has become so ingrained in your psyche that anything other than smooth operations causes you a little bit of mental distress. In any of these types of situations, and others like delayed flights and lost baggage problems, you just wish that you could step in and help and may even find yourself talking to other customers in an attempt to diffuse customer distress.

Number Six. *Always diagnosing service delivery systems.* You mentally critique every service encounter you observe. If you notice that the process is especially smooth, you wonder if there is something to be learned. If something goes wrong, you think about how the problem could have been avoided or quickly solved. You find yourself asking mental questions such as, is the service flaw related to a design or system problem or is it a staffing or training issue? If the service delivery is especially good, you think about what made it so noticeable and how you can replicate the experience in your hotel. As you think about all of these issues, your goal is to find ways for you and your staff to provide better service while working smarter and not harder.

Number Seven. *Constantly evaluating service personnel.* You always notice service employees who are especially attentive and go above and beyond the basic requirements of their jobs. You start to think about how they might make a good addition to the staff at your property and pass along your business card with a parting comment such as, "If you are ever looking for another job, please get in touch with me."

Number Eight. *Being obsessed with occupancy figures.* You seem to always be obsessed with occupancy figures; not only for your hotel, but also for every hotel property you observe no matter where you travel. Sure, you get occupancy figures for other properties in your chain, and you probably even get industry figures from one of the subscription services, but your preoccupation for occupancy goes further than this. For example, when you pass the parking lot of a hotel, you mentally note how many cars you see and immediately convert this into an occupancy estimate. You will even find yourself taking this mental calculation a bit further and thinking to yourself things like "they are probably just breaking-even," or "they will be having a good night," or "they will be lucky to even meet payroll with that level of occupancy."

Number Nine. *Constantly realizing that the hotel business really is a small world.* When you are introduced to someone and you find out they are in the hotel business, you immediately start talking about where you have worked and who you know. It doesn't take long before find out that both of you have a common acquaintance in the business. The hotel business has often been referred to as a very large sorority or fraternity and there are only a few degrees of separation among the people who work in the industry. After establishing a common bond, the conversation almost always moves into stories and experiences that solidify this kinship.

Number Ten. *Work doesn't seem like work.* Filling out reports and responding to requests from regional or corporate offices may seem like work, but interacting with guests and staff doesn't seem like work. You would rather be interacting with people than sitting behind a desk filling out reports. Each day seems like the start of a new adventure and it doesn't seem to matter that you often find yourself stopping by the hotel for a few hours even on your day off. Days and hours don't mean anything when serving guests is a passion and not a job. Each day finds you thinking about your guests and how your team can improve the guest experience.

You can probably think of more specific examples that could set you apart as a hotelier, but one thing is for sure: Any time you are in a service setting, you become a little bit uneasy and maybe even nervous when things don't seem to be going smoothly. You are especially uncomfortable when you cannot identify a supervisor or manager that is trying to get the problem solved and get things "back on track" and functioning smoothly.

Just for the fun of it, think about your own experiences to this point in your career. Now, in the spaces provided below, write down one or two hotelier habits that are common to you or that you have seen in others and pass this book along to someone else.

_____

_____

_____

_____

_____

Maybe we will meet somewhere in the future and can share some of our common adventures and acquaintances. Never stop learning!

www.ingramcontent.com/pod-product-compliance
Lightning Source LLC
Chambersburg PA
CBHW071419180526
45170CB00001B/154